Mountains Don't Care, But We Do

Mountains Don't Care, But We Do

*An Early History
of Mountain Rescue
in the Pacific Northwest
and the Founding of the
Mountain Rescue Association*

Dee Molenaar

MOUNTAIN RESCUE ASSOCIATION

Mountains Don't Care, But We Do
© 2009 Dee Molenaar

PUBLISHED BY:
   Mountain Rescue Association | www.mra.com

BOOK PRODUCED BY:
   Boulder Bookworks, Boulder, Colorado | www.boulderbookworks.com
      COPYEDITING: Michelle Myers
      DESIGN AND PRODUCTION: Alan Bernhard

DISTRIBUTED TO THE BOOK TRADE BY:
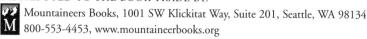 Mountaineers Books, 1001 SW Klickitat Way, Suite 201, Seattle, WA 98134
800-553-4453, www.mountaineerbooks.org

COVER PHOTO: Demonstration of crevasse rescue in 1952.
   Dee Molenaar (litter attendant) with Wolf Bauer and Ome Daiber (lifting).
   Photo courtesy of The Spring Trust for Trails.

First Edition

ISBN 978-0-615-29324-0

Printed in the United States of America

To those who give their time,
energy, and technical skills
that others may live—
and their long-supportive
spouses and families.

Contents

LIST OF ILLUSTRATIONS
Adapted from original art by Dee Molenaar

Foreword

Dee Molenaar has written a comprehensive book on the history and causes of accidents in American mountaineering—specifically on Mount Rainier and Mount Hood in the Pacific Northwest. It is a must-read for all present and future climbers. The heart of this book is the story of men and women who climb mountains and, as President John F. Kennedy wrote, are "pushing human endurance and experience to their farthest frontiers." This book also tells the story of men and women who are involved in the search and rescue of fellow climbers and others who get in trouble in the hills.

To claim that Dee has the experience to author such a book is putting it mildly. His lifelong pursuit of standing on the higher elevations exposed him not only to the beauty and exhilaration of climbing, but also to the strengths, and (as philosopher Rene Daumal wrote) "weaknesses, errors and misunderstandings," of those who climb mountains.

I first met Dee on Mount Rainier. Later, I participated in rescues with him and I was rescued by him. In 1960, Dee, along with almost ninety others, came to my aid, and to the aid of my fellow climbers, on Mount McKinley. I was in a tent at 16,400 feet, getting ready to descend, when I heard him shout from outside: "Is the Co-op open?" (He was referring to the company that I worked for, REI Co-op, the outdoor gear store now known simply as REI.)

Since his youth in Southern California, Dee has climbed and hiked up peaks the world over. As a guide, ranger, geologist, alpine artist, mapmaker, and historian, Dee knows his mountains, and he is a most appropriate author for this treatise. In 1953, he was a member of the tragedy-marred American expedition to K2, and, when he returned to his duties at Camp Hale, Colorado, I heard his account of the trip—and noted his frostbitten feet. This was during the Korean War. My brother Lou and I were draftees and members of the cadre in the Mountain and Cold Weather Training Command, for which Dee was one of the civilian advisors.

In 1965, I led a team that included Dee and Senator Robert Kennedy, which made the first ascent of Mount Kennedy, a previously unclimbed 14,000-foot peak in the Canadian Yukon named after President John F.

Kennedy. The senator was the first person to stand on the peak that was named after his slain brother. Our team had a wonderful climb together, and Dee helped make it a success.

When I first began climbing in 1943, my companions and I understood that if one of us got hurt, we had to get down on our own, or with the help of those in our party. No outside help was expected. I recall an incident on Chair Peak in Washington's Cascades when a member of our team slipped on a snow slope and somersaulted into the rocks. The rest of us had to carry him out more than five miles. I was thankful we had alpenstocks (strong climbing staffs), which we used to make a good stretcher, although if he'd had and known how to use an ice ax, he probably would not have slipped, or could have stopped himself by performing a self arrest. As time went on, more people were attracted to the high places, and it often became necessary to call on climbing friends to rescue other climbing friends. Camaraderie developed among those who repeatedly rescued other climbers, and, in 1959, those individuals coordinated their efforts by forming the national Mountain Rescue Association. It became the group to call if someone needed help in the mountains.

Dee's talent for capturing mountain scenery in his watercolors (his sketches and landform maps have also received acclaim) helps the reader visualize the terrain in which climbing accidents, and rescues, occur. His familiarity with climbing and skill as an author impart a terrible immediacy to the stories in this book. There is hope and heartbreak, achievement and failure, struggle and tragedy. And, although we know that the climbers who did not make it back were living life to the fullest, our hearts go out to those who have lost their loved ones.

In the mountains, there are objective dangers such as ice fall, rock fall and avalanche, over which we have no control, but, most of the time, it is human error that causes injury or death. Dee's book provides an important service to all climbers. If we study what went wrong and what mistakes were made in the past, we can learn from those mistakes.

But this book gives a sense not only of the dangers, but also of the adventures that can be found in the mountains. Future generations can explore to their hearts' content, knowing that the MRA is there to back them up. Climbers might feel a kinship with and admiration for those who go out on the edge in nature, and for those who stick their necks out on rescues.

Perhaps readers will be tempted to enter great forests, wander alpine meadows, and climb higher on the snow, ice, and rock. If this book motivates people to get outside into the high country, and helps them do it safely, then *Mountains Don't Care, But <u>We</u> Do* will have served its purpose.

JIM WHITTAKER
November 6, 2008

Preface

When I was invited by Rick Lorenz of Olympic Mountain Rescue to author this historic account, my chief concern was that I have not been active in mountain search-and-rescue activities for nearly a half century. My last involvement was on Mount McKinley in 1960—before the mountain became widely known by its indigenous name, Denali.

But there have been many changes since those halcyon days of American mountaineering. In June 2001, I attended the annual meeting of the Mountain Rescue Association at Alpental Ski Area in Snoqualmie Pass, Washington. For me, this was a real eye-opener in regard to the latest in techniques and equipment. I observed members of a younger generation of climbers participating in demonstrations and field exercises that illustrated how rescues are performed today. Lightweight lines designed to connect cables for rescue efforts were flying through the air across creek gullies and through a football-field-size area, propelled by small cannons. And there were lightweight ski- and wheel-mounted wire-mesh stretchers moving about in by-the-numbers operations, transporting "victims" from the accident site to a giant helicopter. Saturday evening's gala event started with the first official appearance of the immaculately uniformed MRA Honor Guard, and participating rescuers were all wearing colorful patches designating their unit identities. Thus was I introduced to today's world of mountain rescue. And in researching for this book, I have found that there's considerably more involved in becoming a certified member of the Mountain Rescue Association now than there was in the past.

The full history of mountain rescue in the United States would fill many volumes, and there is always a risk that important people and events would be left out. This volume focuses on the Pacific Northwest, the region that gave birth to the Mountain Rescue Association in 1959. Most of the rescues and missions described in this book occur on Mount Rainier in Washington and Mount Hood in Oregon, two of the most prominent peaks in the region. Time and space limitations prevent a more comprehensive treatment of the subject, and I apologize in advance to rescuers who were not mentioned or who received less coverage in this volume than they deserve. I hope that this book will motivate others to write more on this important subject.

The information on Mount Rainier tragedies covered in this volume has come from my book, *The Challenge of Rainier* (1971), and from my unpublished autobiography, *High and Wide with Sketchpad* (2008). However, while researching mountaineering history and rescues in Oregon, I was greatly relieved to find detailed coverage by Jack Grauer, in his continually updated volumes of *Mount Hood: A Complete History* (1996), along with an as-yet unpublished manuscript by Ric Conrad, *Mount Hood: Adventures of the Wy'east Climbers* (2003), which covers the Wy'east Climbers and the Crag Rats of Hood River, Oregon.

In the final days of this research, I came across a 2007 book by Dr. Christopher Van Tilburg of Hood River, Oregon, titled *Mountain Rescue Doctor*. This book provided much new insight into the mostly unpublicized accounts of a medical rescuer in action: from the midnight call-outs and hurried drive to the accident site, to the difficulty of gaining access to the victim over cliffs adorned with poison oak, often in darkness during stormy weather; from properly diagnosing the patient's injuries and providing immediate treatment, to laboriously raising the victim up loose, overhanging rocks to level ground for evacuation by rescue teams, or, if fortunate, an awaiting helicopter.

This book also owes much to several old-timers from the earlier days of rescue missions, whose cooperation and input was invaluable. Those who responded to several video interviews and more fully to questionnaires include Wolf Bauer, Lynn Buchanan, Hank Lewis, Keith Petrie, Dick Pooley, and George Sainsbury, along with Mountain Rescue Association past presidents Rocky Henderson and Tim Kovacs. Rick Lorenz of Olympic Mountain Rescue provided the enthusiastic dream for this whole project, and helped immeasurably by keeping me from straying off the route. Michelle Myers' outstanding copyediting was greatly appreciated, especially being handicapped by digitally corresponding with an ancient author still adjusting to a PC.

And, of course, I appreciate the patience and support of my good wife, Colleen, throughout the lengthy project, for her tolerance of my utilizing the dining-room table as the principal workbench upon which to stack piles of research books, photos, and correspondence.

Introduction

The following chapters describe the background and events that led to the development of mountain rescue groups in the Pacific Northwest. The book focuses on the late 1800s through 1960, which represents the earliest and, arguably, most dramatic era in the development of formalized mountain rescue in the United States. Although rescues were being conducted in other parts of the country at the same time, the special conditions in the Northwest provided fertile ground and a unique setting. Also, the events that occurred during the time span covered in this book set the stage for the most pivotal development in organized mountain rescue in the country—the establishment of the first national mountain rescue organization, the Mountain Rescue Association. Finally, a chapter on the current state of the MRA illustrates where those initial steps in 1959 have led.

CHAPTER 1

Physical Setting of Mountaineering in the Pacific Northwest

SOUND COUNTRY REFLECTIONS

From homeland Alps, I came one day
Wide-eyed, adventure bound,
T'was in the merry month of May
That first I saw the Sound.

Tradition-wise we dipped, then licked
Our fingers at the beach,
A 'hands-on lesson,' father picked,
To prove the ocean's reach.

The 'inland sea' so there it lay,
Twixt mountain ranges white,
Homesick no more, I, to this day,
Still marvel at the sight!

But since those years in travel made,
Through stormy nights and seas,
With ice ax, ski, or paddle blade,
My mind is not at ease.

The Sound has changed, some mountains, too,
At times have blown their top,
As though to warn, with no adieu,
It's time for us to stop.

And learn that runoffs need their space
When pouring snow-melt o'er the land,
And when to end the crowding pace
That threatens farm and food demand.

Sustain an agro-life, we can,
Both from the land and sea,
Provided that in man's lifespan
Some birth-control there be!

World leadership—a vacuum still,
Religious strife, no end in sight,
To nature's warnings where's our will?
Is over-crowding not our right?

So there I go, political,
Showing my real hand?
(No) Just hoping for poetical
Justice, for our land!

WOLF BAUER,
co-founder of Seattle Mountain Rescue
and "poet laureate" of the Seattle Mountain Rescue Council

It is the natural and legitimate
ambition of a properly constituted
geologist to see a glacier, witness an
eruption and feel an earthquake.

G.K. GILBERT (1907),
in Harris (1988)

On August 1, 1908, sixty members of the Mazamas of Portland, a hiking and climbing club founded in 1894 on the summit of Mount Hood, were encamped on the shores of Spirit Lake in Washington, three miles north of Mount St. Helens' timberline. To reach the lake, they had completed a tough thirty-five mile slog from the end of a muddy road that snaked through dense forests from the main highway in the west (today's Interstate 5).

With a late start up the now well-known Lizard Route, on the peak's northwest slope, twenty-six climbers in a line of thirty-six had reached the summit at 7:15 P.M. While the party admired the sunset, a freezing night wind turned the melting surface snow into glare ice. This suddenly beleaguered party was equipped with only two Swiss ice axes, one fifty-foot rope, and no crampons. It took them seven agonizing hours, cutting step-by-step, mostly in the dark, to inch their way down to their camp at the lake.

Several days later, three young Swedish loggers went through the Mazamas' camp en route to a north-south traverse over the mountain. While they were descending the south face, but were still near the summit, one man's leg was crushed by a rolling boulder. His mates dragged him down to timberline and built a fire, and one man hurried for help. He traversed completely around the east slope of the mountain, reaching the Mazamas' camp just before nightfall.

Charles E. Forsyth, of Castle Rock, Washington, then more than fifty years of age, immediately formed a rescue party, which set out at once guided by the young logger, who must have been a superman. The return trip around the east side in the dark was a nightmare of cliffs, canyons, icy streams, boulder-strewn outwash, fallen logs, and tangled underbrush. By dawn, they reached the injured man, made a litter out of alpenstocks, and started up. Ten exhausted men staggered over the summit at 4:00 P.M.

The descent was worse. Keeping themselves and their helpless burden alive was the problem. Their footgear consisted only of hobnailed boots, worn smooth after ten days of mountaineering. They all later agreed they could not have descended that slippery glacier had it not been for Forsyth. Eventually, they got to the north-side timberline, wandered five miles off course in the dark, and were found nearly dead on their feet by a second rescue team at 3:00 A.M.—all this without sleep or food.

In the 1923 *Mazama*, Charles H. Sholes wrote a hair-raising account of the descent, which had remained clear in all the participants' memories for the intervening fifteen years. The Forsyth Glacier is named for the man who brought them down the slope.

Thus was described an early mountain-rescue operation in the Pacific Northwest. It is a typical example of the spontaneous and informal nature of rescues in the early years. Since that daring 1908 rescue, mountaineering—and mountain rescue—have changed a great deal.

This book will trace the evolution of mountaineering in the Pacific Northwest, and the earliest formation of groups dedicated to conducting searches and rescues in the mountains.

Climate and Weather

The Coast and Cascade Ranges and intervening Puget-Willamette Trough are blessed with a maritime climate, with generally cool, dry summers and mild, wet winters. Warm, moisture-laden air masses flowing from the Pacific Ocean keep air temperatures fairly consistent throughout the year and provide moderate to heavy rainfall from November through April. Winds from the south and southwest generally bring rain, whereas winds from the north and northwest bring clear weather. Occasionally, during winter, cold air flowing south from Canada into Washington and down the Columbia Gorge into the Portland area brings subfreezing temperatures.

Mean annual precipitation ranges from fifteen inches in the "rain shadow" of the Coast Range and Olympic Mountains, to more than two hundred inches in parts of the Cascade Range. Most of the precipitation at higher elevations occurs as winter snowfall. Rainfall in the lowland generally decreases northward from Olympia to Seattle, with about fifty-five inches at Olympia, forty-five inches at Tacoma, and thirty-five inches at Seattle and northward. During winter, the lowland occasionally receives a thin blanket of snow, but it usually lingers only a few days.

Geology

The Cascade Range contains some of the most scenic and topographically spectacular mountain vistas in the lower forty-eight states. The annual accumulation of snow on the high peaks becomes compacted into glacier ice, which, over thousands of years, has sculpted the rugged mountain landscapes we see there today. When I settled in the Puget Sound area and began studying geology at the University of Washington, I came to appreciate the great variety of geologic features found in such a relatively small geographic area. For example, in addition to the high, glaciated volcanoes of the Cascade Range, we have scenery in the Olympic Mountains and North Cascades of Washington that emulates that in the Swiss Alps, and that attracts mountain-loving visitors from the world over. Sharp ridge crests and Matterhorn-like peaks rise a mile above deep, glacier-cut valleys. However, except for the high volcanic cones, the sections of the Cascade Range in southern Washington and extending south through Oregon are much less spectacular. The volcanoes rise above rolling forested foothills with few dominating peaks; only the Goat Rocks area bears a few glaciers and is of interest to hikers and climbers. Between the crustal uplifts of the Coast Range and the Cascades is the down-warped Puget-Willamette Trough that extends some five hundred miles through Oregon and Washington. And the semi-arid eastern parts of those states feature a sagebrush desert underlain by basaltic lava flows that, in places, are more than two miles thick.

Evidence found in the igneous, sedimentary, and metamorphic rocks in Washington extends the geologic record back more than five hundred million years, which is still only about one-tenth of the Earth's 4.6-billion-year history. Most of the present-day landforms of the Cascade and Coast Ranges are products of the geologic processes that occurred during the Pliocene Epoch of the Tertiary Period through the Pleistocene Epoch of the Quaternary Period, from about five million to ten thousand years ago.

During the late Pliocene Epoch (five million to 2.5 million years ago), there was a worldwide development of mountain ranges caused by crustal upwarps along continental margins. In Washington, the Olympic Mountains and the Cascade Range were formed, which resulted in a shift in the area's climatic patterns, with the Cascades forming a barrier that caused a rain-shadow effect. This effect decreased precipitation east of the mountains, where semi-arid conditions have prevailed ever since.

The Pleistocene Epoch (from 2.5 million to ten thousand years ago), also known as the ice ages, was marked by worldwide cyclic warming and cooling. There was periodic growth and expansion of vast ice sheets at the higher latitudes in the northern and southern hemispheres. The higher mountains were also covered by snow and ice, and their valleys were occupied by glaciers that extended far down the foothills and onto adjacent lowlands. During these Pleistocene glacial events, there were periodic eruptions of lava, pumice, and ash from central vents along the Cascade Range. Thus were formed the volcanoes dotting the range crest in Oregon and Washington, including Mount Rainier and Mount Hood, the principal subjects of this treatise.

Within the past two hundred years, both Mount Rainier and Mount Hood have displayed volcanic and other geologic activity. Between 1820 and 1854, several small eruptions sprinkled pumice fragments over Mount Rainier's eastern slopes (Harris 1988). In 1963, a huge rock avalanche from Little Tahoma Peak covered much of the lower Emmons Glacier, and during a heavy rainstorm in November 2006, extensive flooding of the Nisqually River destroyed the popular Sunshine Point Campground at Mount Rainier National Park, and badly damaged parts of the park's road system. The area's landscape is continually subject to ongoing geologic processes.

There are numerous accounts of eruptions at Mount Hood and Mount St. Helens. In 1843, Captain John Fremont and his exploring expedition reported seeing volcanic activity on Mount St. Helens while they were encamped at the present site of The Dalles, along the Columbia River. On August 20, 1859, The Portland *Oregonian* reported unusual clouds and occasional flashes of fire on the southwest slope of Mount Hood, activity that was also observed by a couple of cattle drovers camped near Barlow Pass on the southeast side of the mountain. In 1865, soldiers at Fort Vancouver, Washington, observed the top of the mountain enveloped in smoke and flame, and said they saw ejections of rock fragments, followed by a rumbling noise similar to thunder. In 1907, volcanic activity was seen by a party mapping the Mount Hood area, and reported in *National Geographic* magazine. On August 28, the group reported seeing a glow behind Crater Rock that resembled "a chimney burning out."

The fumaroles in the crater at Mount Hood attracted many visitors and were the subject of many studies over the decades since the peak was first scaled in 1857. Members of that expedition reported deadly fumes, and the death of a climber who had descended into one of the caverns was attributed to those fumes.

Mount Hood must be considered a potentially dangerous dormant peak, subject to future volcanic activity. It is also the source of frequent and recent mudflows caused by heavy precipitation and resulting snowmelt; this has caused damage in surrounding valleys to roads, trails, bridges, and homes.

The youngest of the region's major volcanoes is Mount St. Helens in southern Washington. On November 22, 1842, an ash eruption there laid down a half-inch of ash as far away as The Dalles to the east. And on May 18, 1980, the peak came to life with a catastrophic eruption that destroyed the upper twelve hundred feet of the mountain, caused widespread damage to lower forests, buried surrounding valleys under destructive mudflows, and killed 57 people.

Mountaineering Accidents:
Natural Hazards versus Human Error

The mountains of the Pacific Northwest contain a great variety of rock types, which results in peaks with varying degrees of solidity. The volcanoes are notorious for the instability of their slopes of scree and pumice and ridges of much-fractured andesitic lava. As a result, most climbers prefer the snowfields and glaciers as their routes to the summits. Yet glaciers have claimed most of the victims of mountaineering accidents. Forever moving, with their surfaces constantly breaking up, forming crevasses and icefalls, these beautiful rivers of ice are dangerous avenues of ascent and descent, especially during warm afternoon weather. On Mount Rainier and Mount Hood, it is customary for mountaineers to begin their climbs in the early morning hours, so that they can be off the mountain before noon.

Rock fall is considerably more prevalent on the volcanoes than on peaks composed of firm granite and metamorphic rock. On ridges and cirque walls, unstable rock is usually held together by ice in the shadow of morning, and on north-facing slopes. When the sun melts the ice in the afternoon, rock fall becomes much more common. Afternoon periods of thunder and lightning are more commonly experienced on the drier peaks east of the range crest.

It is human error and inexperience, however, which have caused most of the accidents described here. Those factors are the leading causes of mountaineering accidents in the Pacific Northwest. The climbers' ages, health, and physical conditioning are also common factors. Yearly summaries show that parties led by professional guide services at Mount Rainier and Mount Hood have been more successful and accident-free than independent parties.

The Rise in Popularity of Mountaineering

In the mid-1930s, The Mountaineers of Seattle started offering a course in climbing. This set a standard followed in many other parts of the country. There were still strong individualists who preferred to learn the ropes on their own rather than through organized evening classes. But the classes attracted a cadre of instructors eager to share their knowledge, and plenty of students ready to absorb it.

By the late 1940s, following the exploits of the U.S. Army's 10th Mountain Division in the Italian Campaign during World War II, mountaineering became an established, widely accepted outdoor activity, and its enthusiasts were no longer constantly queried with, "Why do you climb mountains?"

CHAPTER 2

A Brief History of Mountaineering and Mountain Rescue

The pioneers of this new age of rescue have been, in the main, members of the Oesterreichischer [Austrian] Alpenverein and Deutscher [German] Alpenverein [alpine clubs].

HANS KINZL,
in Mariner (1948)

The Beginnings

Mountaineering for its own sake is relatively new as a recreational activity, although accounts of travelers who got in trouble in the mountains began centuries earlier. While some records indicate earlier ascents that seemed to serve no practical purpose and thus apparently were made purely for enjoyment, mountain climbing did not become popular until the late 1700s. Among the main reasons for its popularity were the new view of wild nature as both beautiful and challenging, and the Industrial Revolution, which created a large middle class that had the money and leisure for travel. Many of these early mountaineers also were interested in science. As a result, many alpine expeditioners in the 1800s carried thermometers, barometers, and other instruments to document conditions at high altitude. But alpinists were sometimes driven by a competitive spirit that was intensified by national rivalries. As climbers from Europe and Great Britain discovered the Alps, that competitive spirit encouraged mountaineers to take more and more risks in the name of their country's honor, and sometimes they became victims of their own passion.

For centuries, volunteers like those mentioned in this book have been saving lives in the world's harshest environments. Probably the earliest organized volunteer mountain rescuers were the Augustine monks of a monastery founded in about 1050 by Bernard of Menthon, archdeacon of Aosta, Italy. Menthon created the monastery and two hospices located in popular mountain passes to help travelers get through the Alps. This monastery still operates at 8,110 feet, serving visitors to the Italian Alps and the Pennine Pass area of the Valais (Swiss) Alps. These monks became famous for their highly regarded rescue dogs. A line of dogs descended from the Roman Molossus breed, which was originally used for pulling dairy carts, was perfect for the alpine environment because of its thick coat and sturdy legs. And the breed's keen sense of smell and friendly disposition make it a good choice for rescue work. Called Hospice Dogs, and later renamed St. Bernards, they have saved more than two thousand lives since 1707. The mission of the Augustine monks was viewed with so much respect that the groups' founder, Bernard of Menthon, was named the patron saint of mountain climbers in 1923 by Pope Pius XI. (Van Tilburg, 2007)

Inevitably, as more people found their way to the mountains, the number of mountaineering accidents increased. In the Alps and Great Britain, the large concentration of climbers in a relatively small area guaranteed enough accidents to keep teams of paid professional rescuers busy. This professionalization of mountain rescue created the need for standardized training and certification.

Mountain rescue training had to be modified to suit the climate and topography of the local area. In some mountain ranges, bitter cold, dry air is the norm. But in others, a wet climate is more common, making it difficult for mountaineers and rescuers to stay dry and warm. Scottish mountaineers are fond of saying that climbers haven't truly conquered a peak until they've done it in "full conditions."

In the Pacific Northwest, that Scottish maxim prevails, because of the mountains' proximity to moisture-laden clouds moving in from the Pacific, and a climbing terrain consisting of high volcanoes characterized by alternating layers of crumbling lava strata, loose scree, and talus, mantled by snow and glaciers with their crevasses and icefalls. Also, the major volcanoes, Mount Rainier and Mount Hood, are within ready access of the large population centers of Seattle, Tacoma, and Portland. On the other hand, the drier climates and high-quality granite in the

North Cascades of Washington have encouraged climbers to push technical difficulty to ever higher levels. Mountaineers in the Northwest must be adept at the special skills required for glacier travel, and they must be able to cope with the fact that rapid deterioration of the weather is normal at the higher elevations of the volcanic cones.

With the central core of mountaineering and related travel in the Northwest being principally on Mount Rainier in Washington and Mount Hood in Oregon, the focus of this book will be on the climbing tragedies and rescues on these two peaks. As the two most prominent and frequently challenged mountains in the region, they also became the proving ground for a new class of dedicated mountaineers who led spectacular rescue operations.

Mount Rainier

> *In various travels and expeditions in the territory, I had viewed the snow peaks of this range from all points of the compass, and since that time having visited the mountain regions of Europe, and most of those in North America, I assert that Washington Territory contains mountain scenery and quality sufficient to make half a dozen Switzerlands, while there is on the continent none more grand and imposing than is presented in the Cascade Range north of the Columbia River.*
>
> LIEUTENANT. A. V. KAUTZ (1875)

> *Of all the fire mountains which, like beacons, once blazed along the Pacific Coast, Mount Rainier is the noblest.*
>
> JOHN MUIR (1886)

Mount Rainier is among the world's most impressive and heavily glaciered volcanoes. Rising to 14,410 feet above sea level and 9,000 feet above the surrounding peaks of the Cascade Range, it is visible from more than a hundred miles away in all directions. In 1792, British explorer Captain George Vancouver named the mountain for his friend Rear Admiral Peter Rainier, who never visited his namesake peak. As the dominant landmark of the Pacific Northwest, the volcano—also called

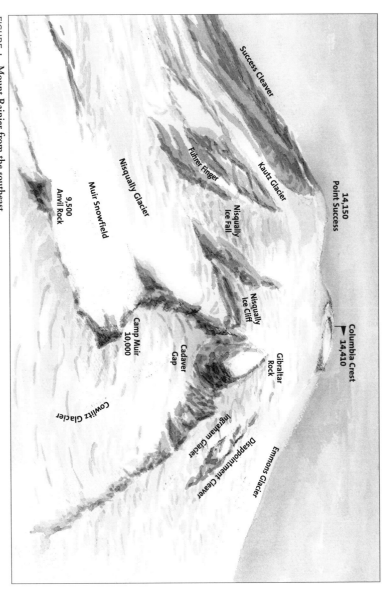

FIGURE 1. Mount Rainier from the southeast.

Tacoma, Tahoma, or simply "The Mountain"—and its surrounding area attained National Park status under the U.S. Department of Interior by an act of Congress in 1899.

With the development of roads, hotels, museums, a trail system, and other accommodations, 380-square-mile Mount Rainier National Park quickly became a tourist magnet that now attracts more than two million visitors annually. They come from around the world—motorists, cyclists, hikers, climbers, fishermen, bird watchers, flower lovers, photographers, artists, writers, and scientists.

The Mount Rainier volcano began forming about a million years ago along the rim of the Pacific Ocean, which is known as the "Pacific Ring of Fire" because of its frequent eruptions and earthquakes. Numerous extrusions of andesitic lavas and alternating eruptions of ash and pumice from a central vent created the peak. This activity was periodically interrupted by mudflows resulting from the heating and rapid melting of the snow and glacier ice that mantled the peak. The continuing process of erosion by the glacier ice modified the volcano and surrounding foothills to form the present park topography of deep, U-shaped valleys, and sharp ridge crests and peaks. Today, these geologic processes continue, primarily in the form of mudflows resulting from melting ice and from the sudden release of large quantities of water temporarily trapped within crevasses and beneath the ice.

About thirty-five square miles of glacier ice mantles Mount Rainier and its satellite, Little Tahoma, the 11,138-foot erosional remnant of the formerly higher eastern slope of the mountain. This is more than the combined total area of ice on all of the other Cascade volcanoes. Mount Rainier has twenty-five named glaciers that range in size from small ice fields occupying shadowed cirques at lower elevations to fourteen glaciers that are more than two miles in length. Seven glaciers originate at the 14,000-foot elevation and flow into canyons well below timberline. The largest is Emmons Glacier, which, in 1983, covered 4.3 square miles on the mountain's northeastern flank. The Carbon Glacier has its terminus at 3,600 feet, the lowest in the contiguous forty-eight states.

Mount Hood

Mount Hood is the highest mountain in Oregon, and because of a general symmetry in its pyramidal shape and its clear-cut, far-seen features of rock and glacier, it has long been recognized as one of the most beautiful of all American snow peaks.

JOHN H. WILLIAMS (1912)

Mount Hood was named in 1792 by Captain George Vancouver for a fellow officer in the Royal British Navy. Being situated within sixty to ninety minutes driving time from Portland, the state's largest population center, this volcano is the state's primary attraction for skiers and mountaineers and is second only to Fujiyama in Japan as the world's most climbed mountain.

Mount Hood came into being about 1.2 million years ago. The Cascade Range in Oregon also comprises numerous other impressive volcanic cones and spires, along with thousands of smaller volcanic hills. Even Rocky Butte and Mount Tabor within the Portland city limits are remnants of fire- and lava-spewing volcanic activity. Mount Hood itself is the product of a series of cones that developed within the general area of today's peak. These cones went through stages of eruption and erosion, and the final cone of today was built by a series of eruptions of lava, pumice and ash in the past three hundred thousand years.

Today, Mount Hood provides a major center for recreation and climbing activity in the Northwest, and its proximity to major urban areas makes it all the more popular. But the mountain poses major risks to the public as well, and its climbing history provides insight into the formation of organized mountain rescue groups.

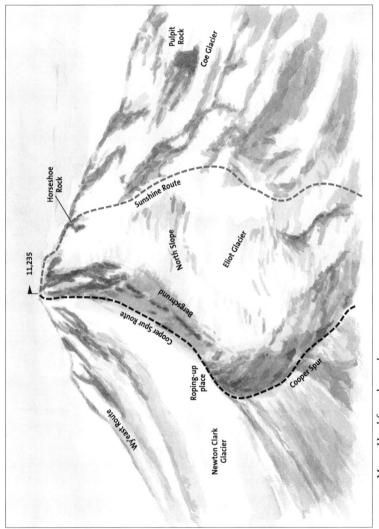

FIGURE 2. Mount Hood from the northeast.

CHAPTER 3 ∿

Early Tragedies on Mount Rainier, from 1897

*Climb if you will, but remember that
courage and strength are naught without
prudence, and that a momentary negligence
may destroy the happiness of a lifetime.*

EDWARD WHYMPER (LATE 1860s)

The history of Mount Rainier from the 1890s to the 1940s includes some of the most widely reported accounts of accidents and their related search-and-rescue activities in the country. People were drawn to these dominating peaks of the Northwest, in part, by their glacier-clad volcanic terrain, which is not commonly found in the ranges in other parts of the continental United States.

The clothing and equipment used by early climbers was vastly different from that available today. Mountaineering clothing of the 1920s–1940s consisted of a "layer system" of warm, often itchy wool underwear, shirts, and jackets, overlain by tight-weave, wind-proof garments, wool caps, and wool-lined leather gloves. At first, boots were knee-length and smooth-soled, with nails driven through the soles to provide better traction on frozen snow and ice. The more widely traveled climbers proudly displayed boots fitted with tricouni nails on the soles and Swiss edge nails around the periphery, items imported from Europe. Four- to five-foot-long rake-handle alpenstocks with metal spikes in their ends were commonly used for balance and as hiking aids. Some expedition leaders, including the guides at Rainier and Hood, utilized the long-handled (36-inch to 38-inch) ice axes of the day.

As is apparent in so many photos from the time period, climbing parties were composed of twenty to thirty (sometimes as many as a hundred) climbers in a line. They stayed together by grasping loops in one-hundred-foot ropes made of hemp or manila, with tested breaking strengths of only a few hundred pounds. But Mount Rainier climbing guides of the late 1930s and 40s taught "ice craft" classes on the Paradise and Nisqually glaciers prior to their clients' summit climbs. They taught individual party members how to self arrest on steep snow slopes by plunging their alpenstocks into the snow. They also taught party arrests, which required a little more finesse and coordination within the usual three- to four-person rope teams.

During this period, search-and-rescue teams did not exist in the Pacific Northwest. The rescuers were generally the climbing guides, park rangers, or experienced mountaineers who lived in the area. The response to an emergency or fatality was ad hoc, and was organized at the scene of the accident. Response time was very slow, and communications were by word-of-mouth.

First Fatal Accident: Professor Edgar McClure, 1897

The first recorded fatal accident on Mount Rainier occurred in July of 1897, during a descent of the mountain by a party of two hundred members of The Mazamas, the area's first established hiking and climbing club, which was based in Portland, Oregon.

After the climb to the summit via the Gibraltar Route on July 7, all but eight members of the party, who chose to remain on the summit overnight, returned to Camp Muir, which they reached at 9:30 P.M. At that point, about half of the climbers were given permission by guide Ed Curtis (who later became a famed photographer of the life and culture of Native Americans) to continue down to Paradise that night. Miss Ella McBride told me, during a 1963 interview, that it was a beautiful moonlit night. She and Professor McClure were scouting a route for those following. At a rocky point, McClure told Miss McBride he was going to work his way down a short cliff. She turned away for a moment, and then heard the sound of a fall. McClure had apparently slipped, or perhaps he caught his yard-long barometer on a projection and was thrown off balance. He made no sound as he fell to his death on the rocks below.

Miss McBride thought McClure might have fainted. She stated that, owing to his exertions in obtaining measurements at the summit earlier in the day, he had become extremely tired, and during the descent he had been continually thirsty, frequently asking for water from the canteen she carried.

The descent from Camp Muir by the remainder of the party the following day almost cost two more lives when W.C. Ansley and Walter Rogers slid into a crevasse only two hundred feet above where McClure had met his death. Although he was badly cut, Ansley worked his way out of the crevasse and returned to Paradise, where he reported the accident. Rogers was rescued by a relief party after midnight.

These incidents occurred before Mount Rainier gained its status as a national park, hence the total reliance on rescue efforts by members of the party itself. Typical of the early tragedies, the response to these incidents was conducted promptly by those on the scene or nearby, with no formal plan or organization.

Forrest Greathouse and Edwin Wetzel, 1929

At 12:30 P.M. on July 2, 1929, a young apprentice guide, Harry Webster, arrived breathless at the Paradise Guide House with news of an accident high on Mount Rainier. Webster had run down from Camp Muir after another guide, Bob Strobel, injured and exhausted, had descended to Muir from the accident site at a crevasse above Gibraltar Rock.

This incident ended up being one of the most highly publicized tragedies in Mount Rainier climbing history. Referred to since as "the Greathouse Accident," the events that transpired over the six-day period combined into a story of unbelievable suffering and heroism among members of the ill-fated party and the rescue team. One guide and a client were killed, and the others in their six-man party were badly injured, when the entire group fell into a deep crevasse following a long slide down the upper part of the mountain.

As they set out to make the first summit attempt of the 1929 climbing season, the party was composed of the following men: Leon H. Brigham, head guide, with forty-five previous ascents of Rainier; Forrest G. Greathouse, apprentice guide, on his first climb of Rainier; Robert Strobel, apprentice guide, with two previous ascents of the mountain; along with clients Yancy Bradshaw of Cambridge, Massachusetts, E. P. Weatherly Jr. of Kansas City, Missouri, and Edwin A. Wetzel of Milwaukee, Wisconsin.

Based on a report supplied by Harry B. Cunningham, chief guide on Rainier from 1925 to 1932, the sequence of events is summarized here:

On July 1, 1929, Robert Strobel and another apprentice guide, Harry Webster, left Paradise for Camp Muir at 9:00 A.M., accompanied by a pack train carrying food and equipment for the summer operations. This advance party reached Camp Muir at 1:00 P.M. The main climbing party left Paradise later in the day and arrived at Muir at about 6:00 P.M.

At 1:00 A.M. on July 2, the summit party left Camp Muir. The six men were tied together on one rope. None wore crampons, which were not often used in those days. The climb progressed without undue difficulty past the Gibraltar Ledge and to the top of Gibraltar Rock at Camp Comfort. Wetzel now appeared tired, but no more so than most of the party. Because of the cold wind, it was not deemed wise to leave him alone, so, after a brief rest, the party continued upward. All party members expressed a desire to continue to the top.

Aside from a cloud cap atop the mountain and a few clouds below, the sky was clear. However, before they had ascended halfway to the summit, the cloud cap dropped down, and the party was enveloped in a strong blizzard. "[It was] the worst that I have ever experienced," said Brigham. "Particles of ice swept into our faces and eyes. It was necessary to chop steps all the way up." Wetzel was becoming so exhausted that Brigham had to drag and half carry him to the anticipated protection of the crater rim, which, by now, was closer than the rocks they had left below. For the last two hundred feet, Wetzel was supported between Brigham and Strobel, who had untied from the lower end of the rope to assist. The wind was so fierce that they all had to crouch low and crawl the remaining distance. They reached the crater at 7:40 A.M. Brigham signed their names in the book at Register Rock.

But the hoped-for protection inside the crater was not to be. The raging wind was extremely cold and the climbers felt themselves growing numb. After only a ten-minute rest, they started down in the following order: Brigham, Wetzel, Weatherly, Bradshaw, Greathouse, and Strobel. From the beginning of the descent, Wetzel seemed incapable of remaining on his feet and continually dropped to a sitting position; he wanted to sit down and slide, which was out of the question. Every time he sat down, he threw the climbers above him off balance. Because the snow surface was so solidly frozen, the climbers found it impossible to get their axes in deep enough to employ the usual method of descending steep terrain (two end men anchor the rope with their axes while those between use it as a hand line). Wetzel complained his hands were too numb to grasp the rope.

Brigham was forced to chop steps all the way down, which further slowed progress. Wetzel was unable to place his feet in the steps, and had to be continually anchored by those above him. Then, according to Brigham's later report, without warning, the man at the end of the line slipped, and began sliding down the incline. The men had been cautioned to dig their alpenstocks and axes in with every step in order to prevent being dragged down if someone fell. But, with the wind pushing them from behind and a fallen man pulling below, it was impossible for the next man to hold, and, one by one, they were all swept down the slope. It all happened in a fraction of a second. The snow was so hard, it was impossible to get the axes in deep enough to arrest the fall.

Strobel, at the rear of the line, was the man who slipped; and he described it as follows:

> I am unable to say what caused me to lose my footing. I may have been blown over, jerked off my feet, or missed a step. What it was, I do not know. As we went down the steep snow and ice, I screamed. Greathouse tried to dig his ax in, but in vain. In an instant we were all being swept down at a great speed. I got but one glimpse of the side of the crevasse as we went over and in. I welcomed the darkness, and the shelter of unconsciousness. When I awakened, my first thought was to get out from under the individuals piled on top of me. Working through the snow, I managed to get out from under them and release myself from the rope.
>
> It is impossible to judge the exact time that we were in the crevasse. It was at least two hours. Nine hours were required to make the trip from the crevasse to Muir.

Strobel said he crawled most of the way to Camp Muir, and lost consciousness several times during his journey, which he narrates as follows:

> We were all in a terrible daze and had to move very slowly. We realized that there was extreme danger of the great blocks of snow and ice coming in from overhead, or the false floor that we were resting on caving through. All about us was porous, rotten snow

and ice. Some seventy-five feet above and to the right I could see
light, so I began working my way up over the grade to what was
evidently a plug in the great crevasse. Finally, I reached an opening
on the lower side from which I could see Camp Comfort. I yelled
to the others that I had found a way out, but I doubted if they
could follow me, as I had better use of my arms and legs than they.
The wind was howling, so I doubt if they heard me. I had to cross
two snow bridges and jump two other crevasses in order to get to
Comfort. From there I worked my way down Gibraltar and on to
Muir. When I was telling the men at Muir about our experiences, I
again lost consciousness.

Once the news of the accident had been carried by Harry Webster
to Paradise, a rescue operation was quickly activated under the control
of Chief Guide Cunningham and Mount Rainier National Park
Superintendent Major Owen A. Tomlinson. Ranger Charlie Browne
was already at Camp Muir, having arrived late on the same day as the
climbing party; he had gone up to make a check of the National Park
Service equipment and facilities. Immediately upon the arrival of
Strobel, Browne had hastened alone up the mountain, passing Brigham
and Bradshaw on the Gibraltar Ledge as they painfully made their way
down for help.

Within an hour after Webster brought the news to Paradise, a rescue
party left on horses for Camp Muir. In the party were John Davis,
Paradise District Ranger; guides Johnny Day, Jerrold Ballaine, and
Nulsen Widman; along with four others. This group was followed later
by two smaller teams.

The first rescue group from below reached Camp Muir at 5:00 P.M.
and immediately ascended toward the scene with stretchers, ropes, and
first-aid supplies. Above Muir, they met Brigham and Bradshaw who,
although both badly injured, urged the rescue group to hurry to the
accident scene. At Camp Misery, the beginning of Gibraltar Ledge, they
came across Weatherly, who had been helped down the ice chute at the
upper end of Gibraltar Ledge by Ranger Browne.

Meanwhile, Browne had continued on his solitary rescue mission.
After passing Brigham and Bradshaw near Camp Misery, and assisting
Weatherly, he climbed through the storm to the crevasse in an attempt
to help the remaining two climbers, Greathouse and Wetzel. After
hearing no signs of life from the deep hole, Browne noted tracks from

the crevasse heading toward the Ingraham Glacier. Following these a half mile down the Ingraham, he found an unconscious Wetzel. His clothing was nearly torn from his body, and he was apparently breathing his last. Browne could not move Wetzel, so, to keep him from falling farther down the steep glacier, he dug a trench in the snow and rolled him into it. Browne took two hours step-cutting to regain the top of Gibraltar Rock before returning to Camp Muir, and then to Paradise, which he reached at 9:30 P.M.

The rescue group that had arrived at Camp Muir that night continued up the mountain in darkness. Lacking knowledge of which crevasse contained the remaining accident victims, they were forced to examine each one they crossed. After three hours of futile effort, the party returned to Muir.

The search efforts were continued the next day when Charlie Browne led another party to Camp Muir. Besides Browne, the group included two guides, Ken Olson and Frank "Swede" Willard, along with Orville Pound, Monty Snider, and Paul A. Williams, a visiting Sierra Club climber. This group hoped to cross Cathedral Rocks to the Ingraham Glacier and recover Wetzel's body.

In the meantime, the first rescue party, led by Day, returned to the upper slopes, found Wetzel's body and started back toward Camp Muir. En route to Muir, Wetzel's body slipped from the grasp of the party and fell into another crevasse. It was later retrieved by Willard, Day, and Ben Smith. Edwin A. Wetzel's remains were then carried to Paradise.

Several efforts were made in subsequent days to recover the body of Greathouse, still deep in the crevasse. It was finally determined that such attempts should be abandoned to prevent further loss of life. However, four days after the accident, Park Superintendent Tomlinson sent a large party of rangers, guides, and experienced Northwest mountaineers to the accident scene under the leadership of Charlie Browne.

On July 7, at 5:30 A.M., Browne's party, with W. T. Hukari of the Hood River Crag Rats, left Camp Muir and arrived at the crevasse at 8:00 A.M. They immediately saw that the crevasse floor had caved in and Greathouse's body was now even more deeply buried in the snow and ice. At considerable personal risk, Browne was lowered into the crevasse. At 8:40 A.M., about fifty feet down, he located the body and, after twenty minutes of chopping away snow and ice, he was able to free the body and attach it to ropes lowered from above. The remains of

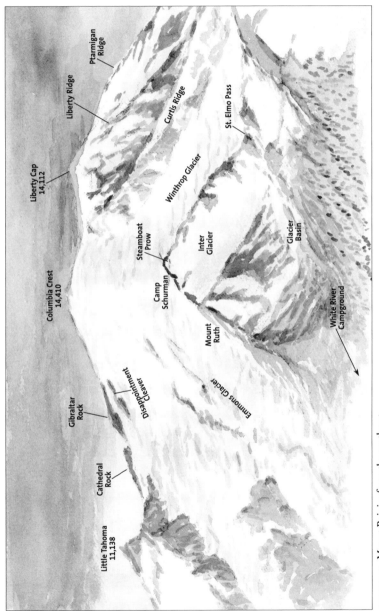

FIGURE 3. Mount Rainier from the northeast.

Forrest G. Greathouse were brought back to Muir, then to Paradise that evening. The notch between Cathedral Rocks and Gibraltar Rock, through which the bodies of Greathouse and Wetzel were evacuated, has since been grimly referred to as Cadaver Gap.

For his leadership in the rescue operation and the recovery of the bodies, Ranger Browne was awarded the first citation for heroism ever given by the Department of the Interior.

The following injuries were suffered by the survivors of the fall: Brigham, two broken ribs, two scalp wounds, cuts on the face, neck, and lower back, shock, and exposure; Weatherly, cuts on chest and buttocks, sprain of lower back, and shock; Bradshaw, broken left jawbone, cuts on face and chest, bruises, shock and exposure; and Strobel, bruises and cuts.

In order to discover the causes of the accident, an evaluation was completed by all concerned, at the request of Superintendent Tomlinson. It was determined that this accident occurred as a result of a party being held together on one rope, most clutching alpenstocks, continuing upward in the face of high winds and decreasing visibility, and the apparent lack of conditioning of one party member. The major result of this evaluation was the requirement that caulked or nailed boots or crampons be worn by both guides and clients on any summit ascent. The use of alpenstocks was still permitted.

This early incident demonstrates that in Mount Rainier National Park, a fairly sophisticated organization had been developed to respond to emergencies. Full-time rangers, with the assistance of guides and highly qualified volunteers, had developed their own mountain-rescue skills. This was also an early and effective use of the all-volunteer Crag Rats of Hood River, Oregon, probably the first volunteer mountain rescue unit in the United States.

Slide into Deep Crevasse: Robert Zinn, 1931

On the weekend of July 4, 1931, a large number of climbers were planning on trying for the summit of Mount Rainier from Camp Muir. To reserve enough bunk space in the cabins, Chief Guide Cunningham sent Henry Swanson ahead on the morning of July 4. A small guided party, led by Nulsen Widman, composed of two guides and three clients, arrived at Camp Muir at 6:30 A.M. that morning. They found both cabins filled, with three or four to a bunk, some on the floor and the roof, and many sleeping in the protection of small rock windbreaks outside the cabins. In all, about eighty-five people were at Muir that night. Widman noted many were poorly equipped, some had boots without caulks, and some had rented whatever gear was available from the Guide House. A few climbers were wearing only shorts.

A strong northwest wind the next morning discouraged many from leaving Camp Muir and only Widman's group and four other parties, consisting of two, three, four, and nine climbers each, left for the summit. Widman's group started up at about 2:00 A.M., following the independent groups that had left at midnight or soon after. It was clear, cold, and windy above a cloud layer at about eight thousand feet, and Widman had to chop steps in places above Muir.

The party of nine, mostly Mazamas led by Clem Blakeney, and the two-man party of Kenneth and Robert Zinn, moved so slowly that Widman's party overtook them. From there on, the independent parties were able to follow closely behind Widman's party. The Mazamas were using a three-quarter-inch cotton rope, with three members not tied in, while the unroped Zinn brothers were following in the footsteps of the Mazamas. Only two climbers in these parties wore crampons, three carried ice axes, and the rest had alpenstocks. As the three groups ascended the chutes beyond the Gibraltar Ledge, a strong wind carried down small particles of rock and ice. A large stone struck Swanson, and he fell unconscious for a few minutes, and suffered a small scalp wound. After a quick recovery, he was able to proceed.

All went well until Widman's party was about eight hundred feet from the summit crater. A sudden cry drew the group's attention to two men who were sliding down the icy slopes. One of them disappeared from view over the rolls of the summit dome, while the other came to a stop. Widman quickly unroped and hurried down three hundred feet, arriving in time to help the fallen man, Kenneth Zinn, to his feet.

Zinn said the other man was his brother, Robert, who had been at the end of the line of climbers. Robert was apparently too exhausted to continue, so he had requested that he be allowed to return to camp alone. After being advised by Blakeney not to go down alone, but to remain where he was on the slope while the other parties continued to the summit, Robert sat down on the snow. Almost immediately, he started sliding. Kenneth attempted to catch him, and slid a short distance himself before coming to a stop. Robert's slide went unchecked, and he steadily gained momentum. We now know that he slid from about 13,700 feet to about 12,000 feet, a linear distance of about 3,400 feet. He struck a badly broken part of the Nisqually Glacier immediately above the ice cliff opposite the upper end of the Gibraltar Ledge. But at the time, what had happened to him was not readily apparent to those who descended to search.

A part of Zinn's alpenstock was found in a crevasse seven hundred feet below where the slip started; then scissors from his first-aid kit were discovered. Clem Blakeney was lowered into one crevasse, but could find no sign of Robert. In the belief that Zinn might have fallen over the two hundred-foot ice cliff, the parties returned to Camp Misery. Swanson hurried down to Paradise to report the accident, arriving there at 1:25 P.M.

A search party headed by Ranger Charlie Browne left Paradise at 4:30 P.M. Included in the party were Chief Ranger John Davis, veteran guide Frank "Swede" Willard, the young second-year guide William J. "Bill" Butler, two horse guides, and a park company employee. This operation would mark, for Bill Butler, the beginning of thirty years of rescue efforts on Mount Rainier.

Browne's party left Camp Muir at 2:00 A.M. Monday, July 6 and traversed across to the broad area below the Nisqually ice cliff. They searched the entire cirque, but could find no trace of the missing climber. They returned to Muir at 6:30 A.M.

On July 7, the search was resumed. Chief Ranger Davis and Ranger Browne became ill at Camp Misery and had to return to Camp Muir. Browne placed Bill Butler in charge of operations. Butler's party continued up to 13,000 feet, and then descended along the approximate line of the fall, looking into every crevasse en route. Butler was lowered into three or four crevasses and found such articles as gloves, a hat, a toothbrush, a first-aid kit, and glasses. Above the Nisqually ice cliff, the imprint of a body was found in the snow surface, indicating a fall into a nearby crevasse. About seventy-five feet above the edge of the cliff, Willard saw a hand in a deep crevasse. Tears filled everyone's eyes as they came to the end of their long search. Using a parka, Willard signaled up and down three times to Chief Guide Cunningham, who was watching through a telescope at Paradise. Cunningham responded with a mirror flash.

Butler and Willard were lowered into the crevasse. They found Zinn's body, badly broken, and frozen around an ice pinnacle. Considerable time was required to get Zinn free of the ice and bring up his 208-pound body from the icy vault. Zinn's remains were left in the snow nearby for the night as the weary party returned to Camp Muir. The following day, Butler and Willard led a group of eight climbers back to the body for final evacuation. While descending the upper Cowlitz Glacier below "The Beehive," a rope slipped loose and Zinn's body slid down the glacier into a 125-foot crevasse. Again, Butler was lowered into the hole for the recovery, refusing to allow any of the others to take the risk. Zinn was then carried down to McClure Rock and returned to Paradise by horse.

In describing the search later, Willard reported that "Bill Butler should be highly commended for his excellent leadership and work. He kept his head at all times and took the most dangerous jobs willingly." For their part in recovering Zinn's body, Willard and Butler received high commendation from the Secretary of the Interior.

The Park Service inquiry into the incident determined that both the Blakeney party and the Zinn brothers were poorly equipped and, although they had registered at the Paradise Ranger Station, no close examination had been made of their equipment. Some of the climbers were observed by guide Widman putting caulks in their boots at Camp Muir the night before the climb. At that time, park regulations required that climbers wear boots with caulks, hobnails, tricouni nails, or crampons, and carry an ice ax or alpenstock.

Information given to me by Portland photographer Ray Atkeson in April of 1969 throws some light on the summit-climb registration procedures in those early days. According to Atkeson, the ranger checkouts were strict, and were designed to keep track of who was on the mountain. Atkeson was in the three-man party that had been in the lead at the time of the accident. After Zinn's tragic slip down the mountain, Atkeson's group helped belay several of the unroped climbers down the ice chute near the top of Gibraltar Rock. Atkeson stated that when the climbers were being checked by the rangers the day before, no close observation was made of the number of ropes in each party. Atkeson thought that this was probably because the rangers were preoccupied with watching, through binoculars, the movements of five climbers high on the summit dome. These climbers had not registered for the ascent. Upon meeting that group of five at Camp Muir later in the day, Atkeson noted they had no rope and only one alpenstock among them, and that at least two were wearing tennis shoes. It was a warm day, and the climbers reported they had no trouble with cold feet high on the mountain.

This is an example of what can happen to inexperienced and poorly equipped people who attempt to climb a high peak. Park Service workers were supposed to check the experience, fitness, and equipment of people registering for a summit climb, which required ropes and ice axes as standard equipment. Apparently, however, the five unregistered climbers on the mountain distracted them from the larger number of climbers right in front of them, who were at least trying to do it right. Again, the rescue was carried out mostly by guides and members of the park staff. This pattern would continue on Mount Rainier through the 1950s, with professional rangers and guides providing much of the rescue capability within the park.

Here is an interesting side note: In a semi-comical adventure only two weeks later, a soldier who was AWOL from Fort Lewis, Washington, complained of a heart attack while climbing with a party above Camp Muir. After a rescue party carried him back to Paradise, he was confronted by his commanding officer. The unsympathetic officer, who apparently had an accurate insight into the young man's character, ordered him to walk from the Guide House to the Lodge, then returned him to Fort Lewis for KP (Kitchen Police) duty.

Delmar Fadden, Solo Winter Climb, 1936

Few mountain tragedies in the Pacific Northwest have held the public's attention for as long as that which befell 22-year-old Delmar Fadden during his solitary winter ascent of Rainier in late January of 1936. The story took weeks to unfold, and nationwide news coverage kept the public informed of events occurring high on the icy slopes throughout the incident.

Delmar Fadden   Photo courtesy of The Mountaineers

At 5:00 P.M. on January 20, 1936, Chief Ranger John Davis received a radio message from a winter seasonal employee, Larry Jensen, at the White River Entrance Station. Jensen reported that a young man, Donald Fadden, had visited the station, saying his twin brother Delmar had not returned from a week of solitary skiing in Glacier Basin. Davis directed District Ranger Oscar A. Sedergren and Ranger Bill Butler to collect their gear for a trip to the basin. Also notified was White River District Ranger Charlie Browne, who was in Seattle on leave at the time.

Early on January 21, Davis, Sedergren, and Butler left park headquarters at Longmire Springs for White River, where they met Donald Fadden. He said his brother Delmar had gone to Glacier Basin to ski, snowshoe, paint, and sketch, and also indicated that he might hike up to Steamboat Prow. Delmar was last seen at the ranger station at 11:00 P.M. the week before. With this information, and after a brief stop at the ranger station, Browne, Davis, Sedergren, and Butler continued on snowshoes to the White River Campground, which they reached at dark. From there, they were able to maintain radio communication with Larry Jensen at the ranger station. They noted that Fadden's tracks went past the patrol cabin without approaching it.

The next day, they continued on Fadden's tracks into Glacier Basin, noting that he had spent a night or two at an old mine cabin at Storbo Camp (also called Starbo Camp). Evidence of food and cooking suggested Fadden had left the cabin no later than January 19. The search party continued as far as the lower end of Inter Glacier, then returned to White River Campground. It was there they learned by radio from Jensen that Fadden had said that his brother was carrying a supply of wands to mark his route, and, with those, might have gone for the summit.

Early on the morning of January 23, the group ascended to Steamboat Prow and discovered two wands in the snow just above that landmark. It was bitterly cold, so they retreated, continuing the search down the north edge of the Emmons Glacier to about 4,800 feet before crossing over the ridge to Glacier Basin and returning to the White River Campground long after dark. They were advised through radio contact with Longmire that another group of searchers, consisting of men experienced on Rainer, was en route from Seattle.

On January 24, Jack Hossack and Bob Buschman, a close climbing friend of Fadden, headed for Summerland Camp to check the shelter for signs of the missing man; Ome Daiber and Joe Halwax set out for the

White River Campground, and Sedergren, Butler, and Browne climbed into Yakima Park. Browne remained at Yakima to observe the summit area with the powerful telescope mounted there, while, the next day, Butler and Sedergren hiked to Mystic Lake to check the shelter cabin there. Hossack and Buschman found no signs of Fadden at Summerland, so they proceeded up the mountain to Steamboat Prow by way of the lower Emmons Glacier. The journey was a long one. They spent a night on the glacier before meeting Daiber and Halwax at the Prow the next morning.

On January 26, Butler and Sedergren returned from Mystic Lake, while Daiber, Buschman, Hossack, and Halwax climbed above Steamboat Prow. They found two more wands, and later, two snowshoes. At 11,000 feet, they began searching crevasses, but an approaching storm drove them back to Glacier Basin. The next day, everyone returned to Seattle except Butler, Davis, Browne, and Sedergren, who remained at the entrance station to await any further information that might be garnered from a proposed flight over the mountain by Daiber.

On January 29th, from a small plane piloted by Elliott Merrill, Ome Daiber and photographer Charles Laidlow spotted the body of Delmar Fadden lying on the upper slope of the Emmons Glacier at about 13,000 feet. The long search was over, but a difficult evacuation was still to come.

A large party gathered the next day to begin the recovery effort. With long delays en route, they arrived at Glacier Basin around midnight. After a short rest, the group headed up the mountain at 5:30 A.M. They were able to travel a couple of miles on skis, but then hard snow necessitated the donning of crampons for the ascent to Steamboat Prow. Above the Prow, the glacier surface was wind-packed, which made for easy traveling, but when the sun went behind the mountain, the temperature rapidly dropped below zero degrees Fahrenheit. The party reached Fadden's body at 3:10 P.M. He was found face down, with his head angled down-slope, and he was solidly frozen. The crampon on his left foot was missing, and his other crampon was partly off the toe of his soft-soled mukluk boot (a boot reaching above the knee traditionally worn by natives of the far north). His hands were bare, he had no ice ax, and his mouth and nostrils were filled with snow. It appeared that he had suffered a fall, been knocked out, and succumbed to hypothermia without regaining consciousness.

Fadden's body was lashed into a canvas tarp and lowered by the five weary, cold men down the steep glacier. The men endured great difficulty while managing the awkward weight, the roughness of the glacier surface, and very cold temperatures. Fadden was continually anchored during the descent, to prevent him from slipping loose. A little moonlight helped after dark, and the group reached the Prow at 7:15 P.M. Fadden's body was left there for the night, and the exhausted party returned to Glacier Basin, all badly frostbitten.

On February 1, a support party returned to the Prow for Fadden's body, which was carried down on a toboggan. The following day marked the end of the long ordeal, as Fadden's still solidly frozen remains were placed in a hearse waiting at the White River Ranger Station.

In the aftermath of the tragic affair, a roll of film found in Fadden's pocket was developed. It showed views across the summit crater, verifying that he had made it to the top and met his death while descending the peak. The cloud and lighting conditions in the photos were compared with weather records from the previous two weeks, and it was determined that he probably reached the summit on January 17.

The summer after Fadden's death, Arnie Campbell and Jim Borrow followed the youth's trail markers to the summit and located his camp in the crater. According to Campbell in a written communication from January 1969, the number of empty cans lying about provided evidence that Fadden had spent several days on the summit.

Because of Ranger Butler's part in the search and evacuation operations, he was given a permanent appointment as park ranger by President Franklin Roosevelt. Several efforts were made by public-spirited citizens to reward those taking part in the lengthy search operation, but, when one prominent businessman attempted to capitalize on the project, the climbers withdrew from further participation.

What manner of man was Delmar Fadden to venture alone to the summit of Rainier in the middle of winter? In 1969, after perusing park records of the climb, I had the pleasure of a visit with Fadden's sister, Mrs. George Gilbert, and his older brother, Gene; Delmar's twin brother, Don was in Alaska at the time. I was given full access to Delmar's photo albums and scrapbooks from the 1930s, and thereby gained insight into the young man's character and aspirations.

During his early childhood in the Seahurst area of southwestern King County, Washington, Fadden displayed an unusually enthusiastic interest in outdoor activities of all kinds, but particularly in mountaineering. He was a talented artist and writer, and was very popular at Highline High School. As a Boy Scout, he worked his way to Eagle Scout rank. In 1930 and 1931, with two companions on each occasion, he made his first extended climbing trips into the Olympic Mountains. The notations in his photo album give itemized lists of the food, equipment, and clothing used on each trip.

The following summer, from July 31 to August 29, Fadden completed a publicized solo trek across the Olympic Mountains. Stating that he was going unarmed "to see things, not shoot things," Fadden started his hike from Lake Quinault under a fifty-six-pound pack, which held all he considered necessary, including a few fishhooks, and a camera "to get close-ups of a cougar and Mount Olympus in the moonlight." To spice the adventure, after his parents had driven him to the lake and departed, Fadden deliberately destroyed his compass and, a few days later, burned his map, exclaiming: "I'm free! Whoopee!" He then crossed several passes and climbed several peaks, including Mount Tom and Mount Olympus, the latter ascent timed for a night on the summit during a full moon.

At the end of the thirty-day trip, he arrived at the mouth of Big Quilcene River on Hood Canal, barely recognizable to his parents after losing 30 of his normal 160 pounds. To augment his food supply, Fadden had stoned several grouse, and, during the final days, he had survived on plant bulbs, frogs, and pollywogs. The journey had its rough moments of near-starvation, rain, and lightning storms, but that didn't drown out Fadden's poetic bent. Playing on the words of a popular children's poem, he wrote the following:

> *It isn't raining rain to me,*
> *No pretty daffodils.*
> *It's just raining misery*
> *With pains and aches and chills.*

Fadden first responded to the challenge of Rainier in 1931, when he hiked to Steamboat Prow from Sunrise Park via Burroughs Mountain. The following year, on October 7 and 8, Fadden and a friend, Bert Kattron, repeated the climb to the Prow. Kattron remained there while Fadden continued alone to about 12,000 feet. Owing to the lateness of the hour, he then turned back, but his photo album clearly shows the icy conditions. He also made several explorations into shallow crevasses.

A week later, following the first heavy snowfall of the season, Fadden returned to the route with Bob Buschman. Wintry conditions, and the fresh snow covering the crevasses that had been so widely exposed the previous week, stopped the two at the Prow. They spent the night huddled in one sleeping bag at the bottom of a crevasse. Fadden's diary notations read:

> Slept at the bottom of this crevice. Cold! Shoes froze (not oiled),
> took half hour to get them on, and he had to warm them in bed;
> gloves like bent wire or steel clamped on ice pick just where I left
> them last night. I slept in one sleeping bag, broke side, wet,
> freezing, snow. What a night; can of half-frozen beans for supper.

Fadden's desire for exploration was not dampened, however. He added: "Bob tied rope to me and lowered me further down in to another ice cave where I snapped this picture. Only little light. Notice snow mound which sifted in from hole above."

Fadden came back to the mountain, again with Buschman, December 26–27, 1932, via the south side. They climbed to Anvil Rock, but were again rebuffed by bad weather. The following year, on September 1 and 2, Fadden finally realized his goal of an ascent to the summit, via the Emmons Glacier.

Because the film from his first climb turned out blank, he returned the next weekend. Leaving Sunrise Park at midnight, he climbed to the Prow in four hours by way of Burroughs Mountain and Inter Glacier, and reached Columbia Crest at 10:00 A.M., exactly ten hours from the parking lot. After two hours on the summit, during which he took a photo of himself by means of a cord attached to the camera, he started down. He reached Sunrise at 6:00 P.M., completing an impressive, though unpublicized, eighteen-hour round trip of this very long route. Though the weather was good on the summit, Fadden included notations in his album that describe making his descent in fog.

> Clouds obscure crevasses such as this one until immediately upon
> it. Fortunately I was following my footsteps. But to come upon
> such a scene further up the Mount is most confusing. You don't
> know which way to follow it. And, as I found, I chose the wrong
> direction back on the Mount, and came near coming down the
> Emmons Glacier (too far to south). Bad business, traveling in fog.
> I got lost on Burroughs Mountain and wandered around for two
> and a half hours.

In 1934, Fadden began his efforts to attain Rainier's summit in winter. In his diary, he wrote the following:

> It has long been my determination to scale the mount, and when I could get no one to try with me, I willingly went alone. Although unsuccessful because of weather, I am all the more confident of future success ... December 27, hiked to Prow alone, deep snow, wearying trip, broke snowshoes, 60 pound pack, slept in snow, very cold. Began hike 10:00 P.M., planned to reach Starbo [Camp] at dawn, but deep snow prevented this ... it seemed hopeless to continue; yet to turn back before I had actually begun was ugly to me ... Reached Starbo on third day after dark. Cleared up, continued to Prow for night there. Returned next day.

Delmar Fadden's life was cut short in its prime, but his soul doubtless would have had it no other way. Many lines in his scrapbook reveal his deep passion for the quiet beauty of dark forests, starry skies, winter storms, and icy heights. Perhaps he anticipated his manner of passing:

> *If a dream meant anything to me, Would it seem a bold reality?*
> *If I knew my hand of fate, Would I do, or hesitate?*

This massive search-and-rescue operation was carried out by Park Service rangers and leading climbers in the Seattle area, many from The Mountaineers. This event reveals the increased reliance on volunteers from outside the park. It should be noted that Ome Daiber and others from Seattle were participating even before the formation of the Seattle Mountain Rescue Council. The tragedy shows that increasingly sophisticated search-and-rescue operations were occurring on Mount Rainier, but deadly results could not always be avoided.

In the mid-1930s, The Mountaineers of Seattle, through the efforts of Wolf Bauer, began offering a program of organized climbing classes, and distributing typed instructional booklets to its members. This was the forerunner of the ultimate publication and worldwide distribution of the club's *Mountaineering: The Freedom of the Hills,* now considered by many to be the ultimate treatise on all phases of mountaineering and outdoor travel and living. There was still no formalized mountain rescue organization in the Seattle area, but people associated with The Mountaineers were beginning to see a need for a group dedicated solely to search and rescue.

Leon Brigham Jr., Unroped Fall into Crevasse, 1941

The tragedy of 1929 was still clear in the memory of guide Leon H.
Brigham in 1941, when his son, Leon Jr., fell into a crevasse on the
Russell Glacier. Brigham and three friends were exploring the glaciers
below the mountain's north face near the Willis Wall. The party was
unroped as they probed for suspected crevasses with their ice axes.
Brigham was leaning over a depression in the snow slope, bracing
himself with his ice ax and the help of one of his companions. Suddenly,
the snow cover collapsed, and Brigham fell into a deep crevasse, and was
wedged tightly between the icy walls. He probably died quickly. While
one of his companions remained at the crevasse, the others ran down the
mountain to the ranger station, where help was quickly mobilized.

Late in the afternoon, a Park Service rescue team arrived at the
crevasse, and determined that Brigham was beyond help. To retrieve his
remains, Assistant Chief Ranger Bill Butler and Ranger Gordon
Patterson were lowered into the crevasse to tie a rope around the
unfortunate victim. He was then lifted to the surface for stretcher
transport to the trailhead at Ipsut Creek.

This party apparently lacked knowledge and experience, in that they
were traveling unroped while exploring the crevassed area of a glacier.
Had they been roped together and belayed, they probably could have
held Brigham to only a short fall into the crevasse.

Marine Plane Search, 1947

After our participation in a successful ascent of Mount St. Elias in Alaska
in 1946, I returned with my brother Cornelius, whom we called K, to
Mount Rainier and Paradise Valley in 1947. K served as a seasonal ranger
for the Park Service, while I joined the Mount Rainier Guide Service, the
guide concession started in 1946 by Bill Dunaway and Bob Parker. Like
K, Bill and Bob were veterans of the 10th Mountain Division.

One of the obligations of the guides was to provide assistance to the
National Park Service in search-and-rescue operations on the mountain.
During a storm on December 10, 1946, a C-46 Marine transport plane
crashed on the upper South Tahoma Glacier on the peak's west side. The
plane had been en route from San Diego to Sand Point Naval Air
Station in Seattle, carrying thirty-two Marines.

Dee and "K" Molenaar, Mount Rainier Park Rangers, in 1948.   Photo by the author

   Determining the plane's location proved to be difficult. Throughout
the next spring and summer, many unsuccessful flights were made over
and around the mountain seeking evidence of the tragedy. Finally, in late
July of 1947, during one of his days off, Assistant Chief Ranger Bill Butler
climbed partway up Success Cleaver and spotted some wreckage on the
lower South Tahoma Glacier. The next day, guides Bill Dunaway, Bob
Parker and I joined Rangers Butler, Bruce Meyer, George Senner, and my
brother K in visiting the site. We found only a few bits of twisted metal
from the plane's tail section projecting from crevasse walls ten to twenty
feet below the glacier surface. I recall Meyer's eagerness to find his Marine
"buddies." He had served a hitch in the Marine Corps during the war.
   A month later, Bill Butler sighted the main body of the plane, using
binoculars. It was high on the glacier's upper reaches, directly beneath
the South Tahoma Glacier headwall. A group of us, including rangers
Butler, Gordon Patterson, and Bob Weldon, again ascended the glacier,
this time to the main wreckage site at 10,000 feet.
   Though the long search was over, we realized that the task of body
evacuation was just beginning. This effort would be difficult and dangerous because of the loose rock falling onto the glacier from the cliffs

above. During the first day's operation, we succeeded in removing about a dozen of the victims from the wreckage, and preparing them for evacuation the next day. We then returned to our expanding camp in Indian Henry's Hunting Ground. There, we met many of the parents of the young Marines, some of whom had come from distant parts of the country.

The next day, we returned to the site with a larger group, including military personnel from nearby Navy and Marine Corps bases, members of the Army's Mountain and Cold Weather Training Command from Camp Hale in Colorado, and a few volunteer climbing friends from Seattle (Bob Craig, Jim Crooks, Fritz Kramer, and Cliff Schmidt). However, the situation on the mountain had changed. Clouds now covered the upper mountain and descended on the accident scene. We also noted that the Navy personnel were wearing smooth-soled oxfords, topped by canvas gaiters. Most of them had never before been on a glacier, but they were all eager to help. However, we anticipated difficulty in having such inexperienced and poorly equipped rescuers on the mountain with us.

But the issue became moot when we arrived at the crash site. Most of the bodies we had removed the day before had been hit by rocks and knocked into a crevasse below. With rocks still bounding down through the clouds, Army Colonel Warren Shelor called a halt to the operation, declaring the risk to the rescuers was too great. Sadly, the parents had to accept the fact that the South Tahoma Glacier headwall would serve as the headstone of their sons' final resting place.

This incident is an example of a large search effort that utilized military personnel as well as Park Service workers and volunteers. By 1946, communications had improved, partly as a result of radios developed during the war. The incident also illustrates the difficulty and danger of operating in a mountain environment and the dilemma posed when inexperienced rescuers want to be part of the recovery effort.

In deference to the Marines' families, the Mount Rainier National Park Service declared the South Tahoma Glacier closed to climbing for a time. A bronze plaque dedicated to the memory of the thirty-two Marines was attached to a large stone at Round Pass, from which you could see the South Tahoma Glacier high above. Annually, over many decades, wreaths of flowers were placed there during a small annual memorial service attended by some family, friends, and park personnel.

About thirty years later, parts of the wreckage were spotted emerging from the terminus of the glacier. I joined a few rangers and local climbers in a long-distance binocular examination of the glacier terminus for possible human remains, but we spotted none.

Enumclaw, Washington's Marine Memorial, located in Veteran's Memorial Park, dedicated in 1999, honors the thirty-two Marines killed in the plane crash. It is an exact replica of the memorial on Mount Rainier, which is accessible only by foot.

May they rest in peace.

The Author's Personal Memories of Mount Rainier

Late in the summer of 1938, after purchasing some food at Seattle's Pike Place Market, my brother K and I left town and drove to Rainier through the twilight. Passing by Longmire at 9:30 P.M., we were in darkness when we reached the Paradise Campground, where we pulled over to the first convenient spot and sacked out on the bare ground. In the morning, we pitched the tent at a site that provided a view of the great mountain rising above the deep, glacier-carved valley of the Nisqually River. Our first hike on the mountain was up to Anvil Rock. In September, the snowfields were covered by dust, and were not as beautiful as they had appeared in the National Geographic ads: "See America First—Visit the Pacific Northwest and its Glaciered Volcanoes."

We repeated our visit to Rainier the following year, again in our Model A Ford. This time we were with two Los Angeles friends, Kenny Spangenberg and George Mayle, and we visited in early summer. The Cascade peaks were all still loaded with snow. On July 9, situated in our large canvas tent in Paradise Campground, we found the mountain a bit more attractive than in 1938, and considerably more snow covered the mountain than the previous September.

At the Paradise Ranger Station, we inquired about obtaining a permit for attempting a guideless ascent of the mountain. After much questioning regarding our experience in mountain climbing ("We've just done Lassen, Shasta, and Hood"), for a dollar, we received the required permit, then visited the nearby Guide House to check the rental price of the equipment. There we met Chief Guide Clark Schurman, a white-mustached fellow in his late 50s; in appearance, he reminded me of General Pershing of World War I. Little did I realize that meeting this

intense little man was to
become the most providential
contact of my life.

Schurman introduced us to
a couple of the other guides
present, whose deep tans
indicated recent glacier and
summit trips. After noting
our homemade ice axes and
smooth-soled knee-length
boots, better suited to
rattlesnake country,
Schurman said he'd rent us
what we needed at half the
normal price. He seemed to
take a liking to us, perhaps

Clark Schurman   Photo by the author

through empathy for our great enthusiasm, which was combined
with an obvious lack of much experience climbing these glacier-clad
volcanoes.

In the evening, we attended a program in the basement auditorium
in the Guide House, narrated by Clark Schurman and illustrated by
hand-tinted lantern slides. Guide Jim Wortham provided harmonica
accompaniment while Schurman recited his personal poetry about the
mountain. We were duly impressed by the feeling these guides had for
their massive workplace.

"Come along, I want to talk to you fellows," said Schurman after the
program, leading the way to the Paradise Inn across the road and up into
the balcony overlooking the dance floor. The rustic interior of the Inn
included large fireplaces at each end; these provided warmth and a refuge
from the fog often lurking outside. Inn guests were enjoying the comforts
of the soft leather chairs near the fire as they awaited the evening
entertainment, put on by the college-student summer employees.

Slowly warming to his subject, Schurman began telling of his work
as chief guide in the summer, and of his principal career as a scouting
leader of Seattle's Troop 65. While he talked, he began "doodling"
with his pencil on a notepad, displaying an artistic knack that I was
to appreciate more in later years. He discussed the routes and some of
the mountain's climbing history, along with a few of the past tragedies

high on the peak. Everything about this unassuming man, and the way in which he confided in us, made us slowly feel at home in this mountain paradise.

Rain the next morning kept us confined for awhile, writing letters home from the Inn lobby until the weather cleared up a bit. After a cold breakfast, we returned to the Guide House, where Schurman spent some time giving us more information on what to expect on the mountain. In the hallway, he demonstrated several mountaineering knots and methods of roping up a party, then rented us some of the equipment we lacked, including a couple of ice axes and alpenstocks, and face masks to protect us from the wind and glare of the sun and snow high on the mountain. We also had a flashlight, a 100-foot rope, and four pairs of wool-lined pants; the rangers didn't like our blue jeans. With our blankets, knapsacks, cameras and food for the two-day trip, we left for 10,000-foot Camp Muir shortly before noon. There, a woman took a group picture of us beside the stone hut—another long-treasured photo that still graces the wall of my basement studio.

A short time later, a guide and three rangers arrived at Camp Muir and prepared for their night in the ranger cabin nearby. They had brought along a couple of large cylinders filled with butane gas, to be used for cooking. I didn't sleep much that night, with my thoughts filled with apprehensions about the coming climb. At about midnight, I rose up on my elbow and looked through the small window toward the ranger hut. I was surprised to see they were already up and moving. Hastily, I awoke the others and we were soon eating and putting on our equipment. The light in the other hut was out when we stepped outside, and on the Cowlitz Glacier, we could see their flashlight lanterns moving and bobbing across the snow surface.

The sky was slightly overcast with clouds, and a slight south wind blew across the rocks as we groped our way outside and put on the 100-foot rope. Kenny led off and I brought up the rear. It wasn't until 1:00 A.M. that we got away and stumbled onto the Cowlitz Glacier. Progress was slow, with the rope strung out, now taut, now slack, as we bypassed several small crevasses. We traversed slightly downward and finally arrived at the ridge between the Cowlitz and Ingraham glaciers.

Climbing up the loose rock, we got to the ridge crest and, looking toward the summit, we could faintly see the lights of the other party, now far ahead. We soon found the rope that was anchored here to help climbers lower themselves to the edge of the Ingraham Glacier below. (This cross-over point on the Cowlitz Cleaver is lower than the one used in later years on the common guide route.) Once on the glacier, we moved along steadily, Kenny in the lead following the crampon tracks of the ranger party. Soon, we encountered huge, gaping crevasses, but we found a way between them. By this time, dawn was approaching, and in silhouette against the eastern sky was 11,138-foot Little Tahoma, a sharp Matterhorn-like spire that is a remnant of a pre-glacial-erosion surface of the mountain. Far below to the east were the twinkling lights of cabins at Sunrise Park.

We continued climbing as the slope steepened on the right edge of the cleaver, amid huge crevasses. We wound in and out, following the others' tracks. But the sky had darkened and become somber, and soon hail began to pelt us intermittently. We stopped before a small snow bridge over a crevasse and looked toward the summit. We couldn't see the other party, and figured that they must be hidden by one of the many lumps and rises that separated us from the thin line of rock marking the crater rim.

Soon, a vast cloud formed over the upper mountain. It appeared this was not our day to climb Mount Rainier, and with George not feeling well, we retraced our steps as the sun was just peeping between cloud bands above the horizon. After taking a couple of photos, we retreated to the lower levels, from where we could now see the other party also descending below the windswept cloud cover. We watched them for awhile—small dark specks against the vast white of the mountain—working one at a time back over the ice ridges and humps.

Upon arriving back at Camp Muir, we waited for the ranger party, and soon they arrived. They were also disappointed about the wind and hail-filled clouds up high that had forced their retreat. It was then that we had a more relaxed opportunity to chat with Bill Butler, the legendary "superman" of the National Park Service at Mount Rainier, whom so many of the hero tales we'd heard from Clark Schurman were about. In the winter of 1936, he had spent five days searching the mountain for, and finally finding, the frozen body of young Delmar Fadden, who had made a solo ascent to the summit.

Gordon Patterson and Butler installed a fresh tank of compressed gas while Jack Broadbent and Bruce Smith coiled up the rope. We then left, glissading down the slopes and making fast time back to the Guide

House at Paradise. K broke his rented alpenstock during one of the glissades, but Clark Schurman said he didn't want any money for it. He finally accepted 50 cents. Schurman invited us to utilize the shower and freshen up in a dank room in the basement. Bob Hoxsey, the Guide House cashier, then snapped a group picture of Schurman with us—a photo treasure that still graces my studio wall and that later appeared in a book about the history of The Mountaineers club.

After a few more days of mixed clear weather and rain, Clark Schurman told us of a group of Boy Scouts who were about to make the attempt as soon as the weather cleared, and he was hoping we would give it another try. But we were running low on funds, and the weather appeared to be too uncertain for us to warrant remaining in the park.

Yet the last morning of our stay dawned clear and cloudless. After loading up the Ford once more, we left our 8-day camp and drove up to the Guide House, where we bade adieu to Schurman. He was shoveling the snow from the path as we left him. How we hated to leave, but we were looking forward to seeing more new country ahead.

The most destiny-directing event of my life was that visit to Mount Rainier in the summer of 1939, during which I met Chief Guide Clark Schurman at Paradise Valley. Then, after I sent him a watercolor of the mountain that Christmas, done in my bunkhouse upon my return to work at my uncle's dairy farm southeast of Los Angeles—and asked if he remembered the four poorly equipped kids in a Model A Ford— Schurman wondered what I was doing with my life. When I wrote that I was milking cows, he suggested I go to college and study art, and come to work for him the next summer.

Somehow, that old scoutmaster had perceived in that thank-you note and painting a youth who would fit into his world of mountains. He took a chance, and invited me to be a guide on the mountain during the summers of 1940 and 1941. Then, after serving in the military during World War II and earning a bachelor of science degree with a major in geology and minor in art at the University of Washington, I served for a few years in the National Park Service at Mount Rainier. Later, with my career in geology, the mountain became the subject of my principal writings and artwork, including, in 1965, a detailed landform map of the national park, the first in my series of such maps of scenic areas of the Pacific Northwest and beyond.

CHAPTER 4

Mountain Rescue Missions in Washington: 1948–1959

The violent and numbing reality of . . .
plunging down a mountainside is in
fact so brutal that there is no time for
fear. More often than not it is an
experience of deep calm resignation, an
utter helplessness so profound that
knowing we can do nothing leaves us
emotionally empty.

JOE SIMPSON,
in Simpson (1993)

After the end of World War II, the efficacy of mountain search-and-rescue operations in the Pacific Northwest was notably upgraded by the return of veterans, especially those of the Army's 10th Mountain Division. With many of these individuals enrolling on the GI Bill in the universities of the Northwest, there was a readily available cadre of experienced rescuers. Most of these individuals also had military experience, and were accustomed to the taking and giving of orders, an official chain of command, and working in well-organized groups, all of which would be necessary in a rescue unit. Many of these veterans soon acquired, from local military-surplus stores, the winter clothing and equipment designed for use on the battlefields of Europe. Chief among the protagonists initiating organized mountain rescue units were Rainier climbing veteran Ome Daiber, along with Wolf Bauer and Dr. Otto Trott, two 1930s immigrants from Germany.

From this point on, there was slow and steady progress in the transition from the random and unorganized responses to emergencies that had been the rule before, to specialized rescue groups that could train and respond as a unit.

Robert Thorson, 1948

An early rescue unit, the Seattle Mountain Rescue Council, was called out on its first official mission in early October of 1948 on The Brothers in the Olympic Mountains. Via telephone, the team was called out by Ome and Matie Daiber to prepare for a climb up The Brothers to the accident site high on the south slope. Robert Thorson, the student-body president of the nearby Bremerton High School, along with several friends, had begun his descent from the summit via a shortcut directly down the south face, but, because of an incomplete set of nails in worn boots, he slipped and fell down the cliffs onto the top of a heather slope.

Ome Daiber, Wolf Bauer, Dr. Otto Trott, Chet Ullin, Lou Whittaker, K, and I drove to the Lena Lake Trailhead in the Olympic Mountains. After hiking past Lena Lake, we ascended a tributary valley and, by sunrise, had reached the accident site only to find a state patrolman there alone with the body. Fresh snowfall on the peak had made him hesitant to descend alone in his smooth-soled shoes. K, Lou, and I placed Thorson into a sleeping bag and onto a wire-mesh litter. We then

Dr. Otto Trott (left) and Ome Daiber in 1948 at the first Seattle Mountain Rescue Council mission—the recovery of Robert Thorson.   Photo by the author

roped him and the state patrolman down to a nearby broad snow slope, where others assisted in bringing both of them to the woods below. By then, a packer had arrived with horses, and the victim was tied across one of them. The rest of the descent was by headlamps. Once we reached the thicker timber below, it became a struggle to keep Thorson's body on the horse. At one point, it slipped and hung below the horse's belly.

Seattle Mountain Rescue Council Truck. From left: Wolf Bauer, Max Eckenburg, Ome Daiber, and Dr. Otto Trott. Photo courtesy of Mike Norman

The litters of that time were made of wire mesh supported in a frame of metal. During this evacuation down rocky gullies en route to the horses, the wire mesh was worn completely through. Had the victim still been alive, this would have caused further injuries. Since 1948, the use of plastics and other lightweight material has made possible the development of litters that are much stronger, and also more abrasion resistant.

James Carter, Lost on Mount St. Helens, 1950

During April of 1950, James Carter was with a group of Northwest skiers and ski patrolmen who had just made a ski climb and descent of Mount St. Helens. Upon their return to their cars at timberline, they discovered that Carter was no longer with them. Knowing that Carter was diabetic and might have become disoriented during his descent if his blood sugar was too low, several group members returned to the mountain in an attempt to find him. All they found were his ski tracks descending toward the east flank of the peak, ninety degrees from the normal route.

Among those called out to search the northeast base of the volcano were my brother K and I, Bob Craig, George Senner, and Chuck Welsh. During the search, we noticed several large avalanche tracks, which was obviously not a good sign. By late afternoon, we were descending into

Ape Canyon, so named by some early prospector who claimed to have been attacked there by a sasquatch that was throwing rocks at his cabin. Having brought little food and no tent or sleeping bags, we were not prepared for a night out. As a result, we spent the night lying on fir boughs beside a roaring fire, which we took turns keeping stoked. Dawn came none too soon, and, after a futile continuation of our search, we returned to the parking lot and headed home.

This search continued over the next couple of weeks, but was eventually called off. Carter was never found. Nine years later, during the 1959 mountain rescue conference at Mount Hood (see Chapter 10), some of the participants brought in a weathered ski they had found caught in a brush jam in the Lewis River. This river drains the southeastern flank of Mount St. Helens. Most believed that this was all that remained of James Carter.

Chasing Lieutenant Hodgkin off the Summit of Rainier, 1951

In the late afternoon of April 12, 1951, Lieutenant John Hodgkin of the Army Air Force became the first pilot to land an airplane on Mount Rainier's summit dome. Flying a ski-equipped eighty-five-horsepower J-3 Piper Cub from the straw-covered airport near Spanaway, Hodgkin landed on the fourteen-thousand-foot saddle between Point Success and Columbia Crest. After landing, he shut off his engine and hiked to the crater rim. But, when Hodgkin returned to his plane, he was unable to get it started. The spark plugs were apparently frozen. He was forced to spend the night inside the plane. Because of the high winds, he was, at times, literally flying the plane as it hovered just above the ground attached to ropes tied to small sheets of plywood he had driven into the snow.

Hearing of this pilot's unauthorized landing atop Rainier and of his inability to leave the summit, the Park Service organized a rescue effort headed by Assistant Chief Ranger Bill Butler. I was in the party, which also included Rangers Elvin R. Johnson and Delmer Armstrong. Our group left Paradise at 2:30 A.M. on April 13. Following the most direct line to the summit, we ascended Fuhrer Finger in ideal snow conditions. We didn't arrive at Hodgkin's landing site until 4:00 P.M. This was, unfortunately, about a half hour after he had taken off in a powerless glide above the steep slopes of the upper Tahoma Glacier. He landed on snow- and ice-covered Mowich Lake, located in the northwestern corner of the park. He was greeted there by Ranger Aubrey Haines from the Carbon River ranger station, who had hiked up to provide him with new spark plugs. Eventually, Hodgkin got the engine started, took off, and returned to Spanaway Airfield.

Lou and Jim Whittaker with collapsible litter and ski in 1958.   Photo courtesy of Seattle Museum of History and Industry

Back on the summit, our team scouted the slopes for items of equipment and other supplies that had been dropped to us by planes from McChord Air Force Base. We bivouacked on the open saddle between Point Success and the summit crater and spent a chilly night contemplating the stars from our frost-mantled cocoons. Our efforts were not without their rewards, however, since we descended the next morning heavily laden with the new cold-weather gear that had been dropped by the supply planes. Once below Fuhrer Finger, we found the skis we had cached the previous morning, and we enjoyed a fine ski run back to Paradise.

Hodgkin was tried by the Park Commissioner at park headquarters in Longmire for his illegal landing of an aircraft inside the park. He was fined $350 and given a suspended six-month sentence. The commissioner was only slightly amused by the contention of Hodgkin's attorney that the pilot had not landed on the mountain proper, but rather on a snow surface that was only a transitory part of the park landscape.

This was the only time an airplane has landed on and taken off from the summit of Mount Rainer. Other light planes have crashed on the mountain's upper snow dome, most with fatal results. This incident is a classic example of search-and-rescue operations within the park during the 1950s, initially organized and carried out by rangers and guides, and supplemented, as necessary, by experienced volunteers from the Seattle Mountain Rescue Council. By this time, an improved call-out system for volunteers had been established.

Richard Mizuhata, 1956

C. R. "Butch" Farabee's *Death, Daring and Disaster* (1998) describes an extensive multi-day search for a lost Boy Scout in Mount Rainier National Park. On August 19, 1956, thirteen-year-old Richard Mizuhata became separated from his party during a Scouting hike in the Carbon River area of the park. While hiking back to the group's base camp that afternoon, Richard had trouble keeping up with the other party members. While skirting the trail's many difficult icy patches and scrambling down a slick slope, he mistook a lower path for a shortcut back to the main trail, but the trail soon faded out. Now frightened, he quickly ate what little food he had left and spent that first night burrowed deeply in his sleeping bag. The next day, he lost his backpack over a cliff. Unable to retrieve his equipment, he spent the next several days moving downhill. In spite of the fairly mild weather, Richard shivered through the nights. On day six, it started to rain. The water running underneath him went unnoticed, because he was already soaked and hypothermic.

While planning the search effort for the lost boy, Assistant Chief Ranger Bill Butler learned that Richard was unable to signal to searchers, and that, if the boy lost his glasses, he would be almost blind. Compounding the ranger's fears was the fact that the lost teenager also had a speech difficulty, which might prevent him from calling for help. Gil Blinn, a park laborer, remembers hiking fifteen miles that first day, and searching for seventeen hours every day for the next week. It was the first of hundreds of rescues during Blinn's forty-year Park Service career that included serving as superintendent at both Mount McKinley and Mount Lassen National Parks.

One of the Coast Guard choppers had a loudspeaker installed on it. If the helicopter couldn't land, the crew could show Richard the way to a landing zone, or, failing that, give him directions to the river, so that he could follow it out. This was the first use of helicopters for a search effort in Mount Rainier National Park.

Bloodhounds were brought in, but couldn't pick up a scent. Seattle Mountain Rescue Council members, along with dozens of other local volunteers, provided most of the ground support, while the military supplied equipment and additional manpower. People from Seattle's Japanese community flocked to the mountain, to help look for one of their own. By official estimates, more than three hundred people were involved in the search. This was one of the largest search missions in the park's history.

Finally, Japanese volunteer Paul Uno discovered the boy. "I saw a place that looked like a likely spot. It was very steep. I just had a hunch. Richard heard me sliding down through the brush. He woke up. I heard him shout," Uno said. That Sunday, after a search lasting seven very long days, Paul Uno experienced the thrill of a lifetime when he located the Scout.

During the subsequent evaluation of the near-tragedy, it was determined that Richard had probably heard and seen searchers moving about near him, but was too frightened to shout and alert them to his presence. The incident is an example of a party's failure to keep all members in sight and accounted for, recognize beforehand the significance of the young Scout's disabilities, and make sure everyone carried extra food and warm, waterproof clothing.

The Mizuhata search demonstrates the increasing sophistication of the rescue operations taking place on Mount Rainier. And it made rescuers aware of the challenges involved in managing a large number of volunteers with different skill levels.

Roy Harniss Rescue, 1956, Olympic National Park

In 1956, a party consisting of Roy Harniss, Jack Newman, "Punk" Cameron, Al Murdoch and Jimmy Richardson set out to climb in the Sawtooth Pinnacles area of Olympic National Park. Harniss was 20 years old at the time. He fell hundreds of feet and suffered a broken leg near Flapjack Lake. After Harniss fell, the party did a good job of patching him up, utilizing their first aid knowledge and a traction splint. Newman and another group member hiked out in the dark, while the others stayed and ministered to Harniss, who apparently had a sleeping bag with him. An account of the incident was provided by Keith Spencer of Olympic Mountain Rescue.

After the hike out, Jack Newman initially called the Mason County Sheriff, who refused to provide any help, or even any advice on what to do. Jack got mad, hung up, and called George Martin, who taught the climbing course at Olympic College. He immediately called the Seattle Mountain Rescue Council, and then began a call-out of college climbing class members from Bremerton. They did not have a stretcher, and there was no doctor, so both had to come from Seattle. This was one of the first missions in the mountains for the Coast Guard, which sent a helicopter from Port Angeles. After Harniss was helped off the mountain, he became involved in mountain rescue himself, and was one of the founding members of the national Mountain Rescue Association.

Keith Spencer of Olympic Mountain Rescue met with Roy Harniss in Sequim, Washington, in 2008 and obtained the photo below. Note that the man with the leather jacket and inflatable life vest (probably the pilot) has a mountain rescue patch on his jacket. The chopper, a Sikorsky HO4S, is from Port Angeles.

By 1956, the Seattle climbers all knew the Bremerton climbers, in part because of George Martin's Olympic College basic mountaineering class in Bremerton. Ome Daiber regularly attended lectures for many years when Martin was the lead instructor. According to Martin, Ome would climb up on a desk during class and stomp his feet and yell "Climbing is fun."

This early rescue in the Olympic Mountains utilized the combined resources of the Seattle Mountain Rescue Council and local climbers from

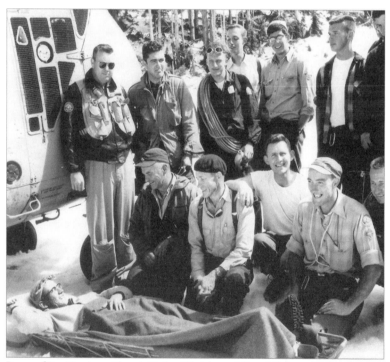

Rescue of Roy Harniss at Olympic National Park in 1956. From left, front row, kneeling: George Martin, Ome Daiber, Paul Williams, Gordy Sinrud, and Floyd Armstead; back row, standing: unnamed pilot, Ray Curtis (USFS ranger), Chuck Williams, unknown, unknown, and Frank Cameron.

Photo courtesy of Roy Harniss

the Bremerton area. It was a good test of the cooperation among volunteers that led to the formation of Olympic Mountain Rescue.

Bill Haupert, Collapse of Rainier Crevasse Bridge, 1957

During Labor Day weekend in 1957, ours was to have been the last guided climb of the summer at Mount Rainier. The weather was favorable, and the route up the Ingraham Glacier, beyond Camp Muir, had been in good shape for the many parties using it since early summer. Guide Gary Rose was to lead the party, and I went along to assist him.

Our party of twelve left Camp Muir at 2:30 A.M., and, even though it included several inexperienced people, we moved up the mountain rapidly. By about 8:30 A.M., we had climbed to the thirteen-thousand-foot level above Disappointment Cleaver, about an hour and a half below the crater rim. Several steep rolls in the summit ice dome were crossed as we followed the wide, well-marked track. Gary Rose was leading the first roped group up one of these rolls, which was about fifty feet high and at an angle of about thirty degrees, when, suddenly, the entire slope shuddered. Glancing up, I saw the lower half of the steep roll breaking up and dropping into a broad chasm. Rose and his young client, Bill Haupert, disappeared amidst the falling blocks of snow and ice. The rope tightened around two other clients on the same rope, but they dug their axes into the snow and didn't fall. I unroped and hurried to the lower edge of a crevasse, all the while calling for Gary and Bill. Gary's voice came back, saying he was all right, but that Haupert was partially buried.

The crevasse was about one hundred to one hundred and fifty feet long and fifteen feet across, with its upper wall about fifteen to twenty feet above the lower lip. Fallen ice blocks filled the hole to within a few feet of its lower lip. By the time I reached the crevasse, Rose had already freed himself from the snow and was hurriedly digging with his hands at a block of ice that covered Haupert; only his arm was showing. In a few minutes, he had uncovered Haupert's head and upper body. Haupert was bleeding slightly at the mouth, but was conscious and said he had a couple of broken teeth. He also complained that his neck hurt and asked us to support both his neck and head. He had no feeling in his legs, and asked that they be straightened out once he was free of the debris.

Fortunately, our party included Seattle physician Dr. J.H. Lehmann, and, with two others, he climbed into the crevasse. His examination

Ome Daiber on Mount Rainier in 1940.

Photo by the author

revealed that Haupert had suffered a broken back and damaged spinal cord. Because the upper lip of the crevasse hung menacingly over us, we deemed it wise to remove Haupert to safer ground on the slope below. A pack frame was placed beneath his back and we carefully carried him from the crevasse and placed him in a shallow trough dug in the snow. Dr. Lehmann administered one capsule of morphine and Haupert soon dozed off. It was 8:50 A.M., about twenty minutes after the accident.

A stretcher evacuation and more manpower were deemed necessary, so Fred Tuttle and I hurried down to Camp Muir, en route meeting other climbers who had by now heard of the accident and had hastened up the mountain to render aid in the form of a tent, sleeping bags, clothing, a stove, and food. At Camp Muir, we sent a radio message to Park Headquarters at Longmire requesting helicopter assistance, if possible, near the 13,000-foot level, or an airdrop of a stretcher. Park headquarters staff immediately telephoned Ome Daiber of the Seattle Mountain Rescue Council, who in turn contacted the U.S. Coast Guard Air-Sea Rescue Unit for information on helicopters capable of attaining an altitude of 13,000 feet. Unfortunately, none were available at the time. Fixed-wing aircraft were then assigned to drop the requested equipment.

Meanwhile, a ranger-guided group started up from Paradise. The party at the crevasse was joined by this group and a tent was set up over Haupert. At 2:30 P.M., after leaving Dr. Lehmann and one of the climbers from the other party with Haupert, Rose led the remainder of his clients back to Camp Muir. En route, he rejoined me and an advance rescue team that had come up from Paradise, led by chief guide Dick McGowan. As we started back up the glacier, we met two members of a party of four Austrian climbers who said their other two members had retrieved one of the stretchers dropped on the upper slopes by a circling U.S. Coast Guard plane.

Soon after, we met the other two Austrians, who gave us the sad news that Haupert had passed away a short time earlier. The evacuation of Haupert's remains involved members of the guide service, Park Service, and Seattle Mountain Rescue Council. By now, the organized volunteer teams were making a major contribution to mountain rescue in the Pacific Northwest.

Deaths at the Rainier Summit, 1959

In late August of 1959, Dr. Calder T. "Tup" Bressler, Professor of Geology at Western Washington State College (now University) in Bellingham, was invited by Dr. Maynard Miller, Director of the study "Project Crater," to visit the summit camp on Rainier. Bressler had been active during the summer and had no trouble reaching the summit. While at Camp Muir, during Bressler's night there on August 30, I had the pleasure of meeting this fellow geologist for the first time.

The next afternoon, after a night spent at the tent camp on the crater rim, Bressler complained of feeling weak. He went to bed early. At 4:30 A.M., tent mate Barry Prather noted that Bressler was groaning. It was apparent that he was suffering the early symptoms of pulmonary edema. Oxygen was administered at the camp, but, by afternoon, Bressler had lapsed into a coma.

Late in the evening of September 1, pilot Harold Horn, who had been air-dropping supplies to the camp during the summer, prepared to drop some oxygen cylinders at the summit camp. With him was fellow pilot Charles Carman. After a late start from the airport, they were finally circling the summit of the peak near twilight. The accident was not observed by those in camp, but, when the plane failed to make the drop, a message was radioed down the mountain. It's possible that a sudden downdraft, coupled with fading visibility, was what caused the small plane to dive into the summit immediately east of Point Success.

At dawn the following day, Bressler quietly passed away. Evacuation of his body soon began, but a storm struck the party on the Ingraham Glacier, and Bressler had to be left while the group descended to Camp Muir. Over the next week, the storm continued unabated, covering both the aircraft and Bressler. During a brief clearing, a party returned to the

Ingraham Glacier and, after considerable probing, found Bressler's remains beneath four feet of fresh snow. The remains were transported to Paradise.

Nearly a week passed before the weather cleared sufficiently to allow a search for the aircraft. It was first spotted from the air. Just a few inches of one of the tires was showing above the flat surface of the summit snowfield near Point Success. I accompanied a ground party led by Bill Butler that included Maynard Miller and several other members of his crater-study project. The crashed plane was found on its back, buried beneath the snow. Dave Mahre dug down to the cabin and found the occupants frozen solid. I then descended into the cabin to retrieve a few personal effects. Under these conditions, we decided to leave the bodies and crash site as they were.

The practice of leaving the remains of mountaineering tragedies at or near the accident site is not unusual. Even the victims' family members have indicated no desire to endanger the lives of rescuers in the process of evacuating their loved one's remains from hazardous terrain.

CHAPTER 5

Early Tragedies on Mount Hood, from 1896–1943

These two gullies above the Eliot Glacier are the most difficult routes on the mountain, along with Yokum Ridge on the northwest flank ... [and] to the east the difficult and dangerous Cooper Spur Route.

DR. CHRISTOPHER VAN TILBURG,
in Van Tilburg (2007)

The base of the southern slope of Mount Hood, the area served by the Timberline Lodge complex, is the most visited of all the skiing and climbing areas in Oregon. An estimated ten thousand people per year register to scale this peak. Hence, Mount Hood has a history of many deaths and injuries, with more than one hundred people killed on its slopes in the past one hundred years. Many climbers attempt this peak during the May and June "busy season." Unfortunately, lack of experience, improper training, and poor equipment are common.

I've always considered Mount Hood in Oregon and Mount St. Helens in Washington as the two most dangerous peaks in the Pacific Northwest to hikers and neophyte mountaineers. Only a short drive from Portland, Mount Hood is characterized by relatively open and gentle terrain at its base. This attracts many weekend hikers and skiers to the easily reached steep upper mountain. There lurk the hazards of steep ice slopes and crevasses to trap the unwary.

The following summary of major incidents on Mount Hood was compiled by Jack Grauer (1996), and is reproduced with his permission.

Frederic Kirn, 1896

Mount Hood's first reported climbing casualty was Frederic Kirn, a Portland grocer of Swiss birth who fell to his death onto the Newton Clark Glacier on Monday, July 12, 1896. He arrived at Cloud Cap Inn on Sunday afternoon, an elderly but vigorous man who had walked from the rail station at Hood River. Scanning the mountainside with his field glasses, he asked many questions of guide Will Langille, finally commenting that he could find the way himself and did not need a guide. Many of his questions concerned volcanic phenomena. Langille pointed out some features to him, warning that it would be dangerous to reach them.

Kirn rose at 4:00 A.M., consumed only a cup of coffee, and left the inn a half hour later for his adventure on the slopes that reminded him of his native Switzerland. Tanzana Langille watched him, occasionally, through the telescope, but she soon lost visual contact. By 5:30 P.M., both Langilles were quite worried, so Will went out to look for their guest. He followed the tracks, which were clear enough, to within seven hundred feet of the summit, where they veered south onto a steep and treacherous rocky area and disappeared. It became obvious that Kirn had trusted a slope of rock that had slid out from under him, perhaps triggered by his own footsteps.

Langille carefully followed the slope of the avalanche for about three hundred feet, fearing for his own safety most of the time because of the high angle of the mountainside. Then he came to the edge of the cliff and saw Kirn's body lying four hundred feet below, surrounded by the rocks that had swept him to his death. It was 8:30 P.M., and the guide, knowing that there was no chance that Kirn was alive, went back to Cloud Cap and called the police in Portland. An officer then went to Kirn's home and broke the news to his wife and daughter, who at first refused to believe the terrible story, then broke down in shock.

It took five men all of the next morning to retrieve Kirn's remains. Getting to his body was very hazardous, because he had come to rest on the very steep ice just above the bergschrund (a type of crevasse). A slide of a few more feet would have carried him into the bergschrund, from where he would probably never have been retrieved. After that, it took six men until evening to bring Kirn down to Cooper Spur, where they could lash his remains to the back of a waiting horse.

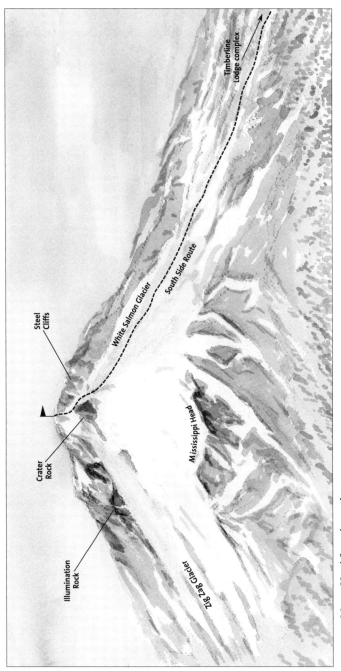

FIGURE 4. Mount Hood from the southwest.

The search effort was initiated by Will Langille, who based his operation at Cloud Cap Inn, near the timberline. There he enlisted a few friends and volunteers to ascend the mountain and retrieve the victim.

Later, Kirn's family indicated that he had long been intrigued with Mount Hood. He had previously been in the hops business near Gervais, Oregon, and, from his home there, he would often admire the mountain. He wrote considerable poetry, and felt he must visit Mount Hood to better put down his thoughts in meaningful verse. So, it was upon this solitary pilgrimage to his beautiful mountain that he met his fate.

This early incident has many parallels to the early missions on Mount Rainier. A mountain guide and his friends in the area of the incident responded spontaneously without any formal organization.

Leslie Brownlee, 1927

"Somewhere down there is Brownlee." Many climbers and would-be rescuers repeated that comment after a fruitless search on New Year's Day in 1927. Leslie Brownlee, 21, and Al Feyerabend, his school friend, sought the distinction of being the first to summit Mount Hood in 1927. They left Battle Axe Inn at Government Camp early on Friday, December 31, 1926, equipped with snowshoes, heavy parkas, flashlights, a compass, and hot food in thermal bottles. The sky was overcast, but weather at Government Camp was above freezing. At Timberline cabin (in the locale of today's Timberline Lodge), they rested for an hour, and stepped out at 1:30 A.M. into the beginnings of a blizzard.

At 4:00 A.M., the two could still see the lights of Portland, but by 5:00 A.M., the storm began to dump snow upon them. At 6:00 A.M., they were drowsy and lay down to sleep, both awakening cold and stiff. With visibility poor, they followed the edge of White River Glacier, expecting to hit the slopes that fall steeply from Crater Rock. Soon, they veered west, then tried a compass course due north.

Brownlee showed signs of exhaustion and decided to turn back, but Feyerabend, in his exuberance, failed to realize that would be his last chance to safely descend. Brownlee turned back on a compass bearing that he thought should take him to the timberline area and Government Camp. Feyerabend foolishly continued upward, pride and fear of ridicule being more important to him than self-preservation. He soon gave up, and faced the problem of descending through the soft snow, facing a high wind.

A momentary break in the clouds showed Feyerabend that he was close to the great, dark walls of Mississippi Head, which meant that he had drifted west, just as so many other climbers have done while descending from Crater Rock during storms. Veering to the east in his descent, he reached the Timberline cabin and was told that four young men had just left for Government Camp. Naturally, he assumed that one was Brownlee, so it was only after descending to the comfort of Battle Axe Inn that he discovered that his climbing partner was missing.

A massive search was begun. Loggers, Portland police, sheriff's deputies from four counties, climbing club members, and many interested onlookers converged at Government Camp to help in the search. Ray Conway, an expert on searches and mountaineering, rose from his sickbed to take charge of the operation at Timberline Cabin. The U.S. Forest Service managed to run a telephone line to the cabin, which allowed communication with general headquarters at Battle Axe Inn, under the command of L. A. Nelson of the Mazamas. The mountain was combed in detailed grids; no area was ignored.

The old Timberline Cabin pulsed with activity as tired searchers came in to hang clothes to dry and crawl into a bunk, as soon as one became empty. Soup and coffee simmered on the battered stove. At Battle Axe, the owner, Everett Sickler, had to abandon business as all efforts turned to the search. Dripping garments hung around the big lobby on the antlers of deer and moose heads, and from the Indian artifacts and pioneer relics that decorated the wall. Men, dizzy from lack of sleep, slumped in chairs or lay on the floor, getting any rest they could. A fund to buy food was initiated by the Portland Advertising Club.

All too few skiers were available. Most of the search was done on snowshoes, tramping through the heavy, wet snow. After a week, Nelson and Conway held a conference with the other leaders. They decided that Brownlee could not be found. For years, hikers and climbers probed obscure niches on the south side of Mount Hood looking for his body.

It is obvious that some of the well-meaning "interested onlookers" involved in the search were not qualified to be wandering about on the mountain in bad weather with inadequate clothing. There was a definite need for better-trained and better-organized people to be involved in these missions.

Looking at the history of these mountaineering tragedies, it becomes clear that the rescuers began to learn from their mistakes. Each incident caused some change in the next response, i.e. better organization, equipment, and communication.

Dr. Stanton Stryker, 1927

On July 17, 1927, a beautiful, clear Sunday, the Mazamas annual climb of Mount Hood was under way. Early climbers could be seen walking on the summit ridge as the party of 103 was led across Eliot Glacier on the way to the Sunshine Route by the club president, Judge Fred Stadter. This was the first time the Mazamas had ever undertaken the Sunshine Route as a club.

Suddenly, a serac (a fractured, unstable block of snow or ice) as large as a small office building collapsed directly above one of the unroped parties that was proceeding across the unbroken middle shelf of the glacier. Don Onthank remembers well the instant terror that ensued, with the thought of the party being buried under tons of ice blocks. Fortunately, an unseen crevasse lay below the collapsing serac, and it stopped the snow and ice before it reached the party.

Soon after, the party approached the Coe Glacier and began to rope up. Onthank had been walking a little behind, chatting with friends, and, upon reaching one of the rope teams, he found that only about four feet of rope was left for him at the rear. Since this was insufficient for tying around his waist, he merely tied a loop in the end and held on.

As they traversed up the snowfields near Horseshoe Rock, someone in the center of the rope slipped, pulling the others down. Harry Krebs tried to arrest the fall with his ice ax, but the initial pull was too strong, and the whole group slid down the slope out of control. Onthank suddenly discovered he was standing by himself, because the rope had been pulled from his hand. Some of the climbers were novices, completely untrained. During the first few seconds, several lost their alpenstocks, while the rest were vainly trying to arrest the slide. For about six hundred feet, the group engaged in crack-the-whip, as first one person, then another, would succeed in partially halting the fall, only to be pulled out of position by the rest. Rope leader Krebs almost had the fall stopped at first. Mary Malloy, W.H. Harris, and Krebs thought they had it stopped later, but the weight of falling bodies on the line pulled them out of position.

The entire group became a whirling ball of humanity as it approached the end of its six-hundred-foot, uncontrolled slide. With screams of terror, they flew over the lip of the bergschrund, falling thirty feet into soft snow on the lower lip. Fortunately, their speed carried them far enough to avoid a direct drop into the crevasse.

Clem Blakeney and Perlee G. Payton had been assisting on the climb, and were ascending unroped. These two, followed by Don Onthank and many of the other climbing leaders, immediately descended the steep snow to rescue the victims. Blakeney pulled Mary Malloy out first; her right ankle was broken and her chest was injured. Dr. Stanton Stryker had been impaled through the chest with an alpenstock. They pulled it out of him and slowed the loss of blood with snow. Stryker was conscious after the fall, and concerned about the condition of the others, but he eventually succumbed to his injuries. When asked if he had any last words, he replied that his affairs were in order, and he was at peace with the world.

It is obvious that more care should have been taken to ensure that there was more than one experienced belayer on each rope. This was also before ice axes replaced alpenstocks and before instructions were given on how to arrest individual and roped-party falls using ice axes. Having more mountaineers and club members skilled in the use of rope and ax living in the vicinity would have benefited the group. Later, in Seattle in the late 1940s, climbing organizations such as The Mountaineers would provide the nucleus of mountain-rescue training and organization.

Glen Gullickson, 1932

On Tuesday, July 5, 1932, Glen Gullickson, of college age, was the last of three men descending the chute on the South Side Route of Mount Hood at about 7:30 A.M. The slope was still in the shadow of the cliffs and very icy. The usual fixed rope to make the descent easier had not yet been hung in the chute for the year. Glen slipped on hard ice, lost his alpenstock, then tumbled and bounced eight hundred feet to the bottom of the chute, where he fell free for about seventy-five feet to the bottom of a depression. Fortunately, he did not strike the other two men he slid past, because he probably would have taken them with him.

Glen's climbing partners descended and found him unconscious and bleeding. One of his companions, Wayne Aden, went down to Government Camp, arriving at about noon. The other, Gordon Nugent, stayed there with the victim. At the Government Camp Hotel, Perlee

Payton, Mazamas leader and guide, organized a rescue group at once. Tom Sherrard, supervisor of Mount Hood National Forest, assigned Chester Jones and Carl Hendrickson of the Zigzag Ranger Station to the job. In addition, Vincent Rafferty, Charles Newell, and Everett Morrison participated.

The previous day's storm had coated the mountain with ice, so it took the party until 8:00 P.M. to reach Gullickson. When they arrived, he was dead, with a large wound in the back of his head, and possibly a broken neck. Bringing Gullickson's body down the ice-sheathed slopes was difficult, and Payton's group moved slowly. Observers below watched the pinpoints of light as the rescuers chopped steps and belayed. They reached Government Camp at 1:25 A.M.

Aden and Nugent later said that Gullickson probably slipped because of weakness in one of his legs, caused by a previous injury. He had recently cut the tendons in one leg with an ax while at the Spirit Lake YMCA camp. He had complained about it before starting.

Again we see experienced volunteer mountaineers assisting the full-time rangers in conducting a rescue operation. This became a common pattern as mountain rescue evolved in the Pacific Northwest after 1926.

Barbara Drum, Struck by Rock, 1934

On September 3, 1934, Barbara Drum, 35, a graduate student at the University of Washington and hostess at Cloud Cap Inn, joined a party led by guide William Moody that set out to remove the fixed rope from the summit area on Mount Hood's Cooper Spur Route. At the end of the strenuous day, Moody put Miss Drum on the end of his rope while they climbed up the Cooper Spur bordering the upper Newton Clark Glacier.

Suddenly, a six-inch boulder came down the mountain and struck Drum in the small of her back, hurling her off her feet. The rope saved her from a fall into a crevasse. The men were afraid to attempt an evacuation from the dangerously crevassed area, and decided to wait until morning. One of them went for blankets at Cloud Cap Inn and relayed the news of the accident. They kept Drum warm all night, but she remained disoriented.

On September 4, they brought her down to Cloud Cap Inn, and on September 5, Homer Roger, operator of the inn, took her to the hospital in Hood River. After a few days in the hospital, Barbara seemed to be recovering, but, on September 16, she suddenly died as a result of her injury.

Roy Varney and Russell Gueffroy, 1938

On Sunday, March 27, 1938, a party of Mazamas left Mount Hood's Timberline Lodge at 1:00 A.M. for the first winter climb the club had ever scheduled. The party of twenty was headed by co-leaders Joe Leuthold and William Wood. They had come up to Timberline Lodge in a bus from the Mazama Lodge. The weather was clear and cold, with a breakable crust on the snow. Four party members were on snowshoes, and the rest were on skis.

At Triangle Moraine, they left their skis and headed for the summit. The weather was somewhat pleasant as they tied in to two ropes to ascend the chute. Leuthold took his string up first, and, as they neared the top, a sleet storm hit the group. The second rope team did not start up the chute, but turned around and headed down the mountain. Although they were only fifty feet from the summit ridge, Leuthold turned his party around. Ice was freezing on their glasses, and a fierce wind drove ice particles into their faces.

Roy Varney, a strong climber and the chairman of the Climbing Committee of the Mazamas, began to fail near Crater Rock. It was later theorized by physicians that he suffered a stroke or heart attack. He was wearing only a cotton work shirt, certainly not sufficient clothing for such an ascent. Dorothy Clark, suffering mountain sickness herself, recalls lagging back to help him. The last thing she can remember him saying was: "My God, Dorothy, I can't see," as she helped him along.

Co-leader William Wood and Russell Gueffroy finally took over. Gueffroy and Dorothy descended to Triangle Moraine, where Leuthold was consolidating his string of ten. Gueffroy told Leuthold that Wood was proceeding slowly with Varney. Leuthold sent Clyde Hildreth and Max Gatewood back up to assist with Varney, who was stumbling and falling. Leuthold's string of climbers then began complaining about the cold, and begged to be allowed to move, so Leuthold sent them down toward the safety of Timberline Lodge. He then started down alone on skis.

Leuthold used his skis so he could get to Timberline Lodge as soon as possible. This would allow him to get the snowcat and return to evacuate Varney, but, when he got there, the keys were gone, probably in the pocket of an operator who had left for town. Efforts to get another set were not fruitful. Leuthold finally became a medical case himself, in the hands of Ralph Wiese, Ski Patrol First Aid Chief; he was exhausted from his ordeal on the mountain.

Meanwhile, Wood, Max Gatewood, and Clyde Hildreth had lashed the incapacitated Roy Varney to a pair of skis. Their progress on foot, struggling through the breakable crust, was very slow. Dorothy, who had left her skis at Triangle Moraine and was walking down, remembers the violent, cold wind. It picked up ice crystals on the surface and hurled them at her face and hands, even infiltrating the inside of her jacket. Gatewood and Hildreth came to the end of their endurance a quarter mile above Lone Fir Lookout. They struck out for Timberline Lodge for self-preservation, leaving Wood huddled with Varney. Wood lasted only a few more minutes, and had to leave Varney alone. The three straggled into the lodge in falling snow that had further cut visibility. They had barely saved their own lives, and were suffering from exhaustion and exposure.

District Ranger Harold Engles was watching the situation with intense interest from the lodge. When Hildreth and Gatewood came in with the news about Varney, he quickly took Max Becker and Henry Corbett with him on skis to find him. Engles told Ski Patrol Chief Hank Lewis to stay on patrol work. By 4:30 A.M., the storm had closed in, dumping a load of new snow on the breakable crust. Directing Ralph Wiese to take over for him, Lewis left shortly afterward, by himself, in an attempt to overtake the Engles party. Visibility was about five feet through the horizontally driven snow.

Lewis groped his way to Lone Fir and, with considerable yelling, finally located the Engles party that had by that time reached the unconscious Varney. Engles had taken two ax handles and wire to lash his and Hank's specially drilled skis into a toboggan. Then came the nightmare of pulling Varney back to the lodge. It took four hours to descend a mile and a quarter. At one point, the party fell down a very steep slope, possibly Salmon River Canyon, and had to climb back out again. Then their path brought them down the ridge above the lodge. Finally, the onlookers inside the lodge noticed their lights on the hill. A group, including Ted Coomara, Merritt Cookingham, James Green, Jack Stockman, N.A. Norene, and William Bookmire, charged out into the night to help pull the toboggan down.

Once Varney reached the lodge, Ralph Wiese worked tirelessly on him, giving him artificial respiration long after anyone else had any hope. A physician departed by Grayline limousine from Gresham, but it stalled in the heavy snow a mile from the lodge. The doctor walked the last mile holding on to the driver's belt. He pronounced Varney dead, despite the efforts of Wiese, and the use of a resuscitator from the Gresham Fire Department. Varney's heartsick climbing companions and the searchers made their way back to Portland when road conditions permitted.

The following day, someone noticed a car on the highway below Mazama Lodge near Government Camp. It was the automobile of Russell Gueffroy, and a check in Vancouver showed that the expedition member had not returned to his home. The search was on once more.

On Monday night, the telephone lines in Portland were alive with calls asking searchers to come to Mount Hood. Hank Lewis was asked to head the operation in the field. On Tuesday morning, Lewis, Leuthold, Bill Hackett, Russ McJury, and Ray Lewis drove to Timberline Lodge, where Ranger Engles had Boyd Rasmussen, Max Becker, and Boyd French ready to go. Gary Leach came up from Government Camp, and veteran search director Ray Conway came to the lodge to lend his expertise. Conway arranged for the feeding of the search crews with the lodge.

The bad weather persisted, so only Boyd French was permitted to be out alone. Leach and Ray Lewis went to White River, with Hank Lewis, Max Becker, and Al Cohn working another section of the same canyon. Ted Coomara and James Green were sent up past Lone Fir. Harry Johnson and Jack Ferrell searched in the Salmon River Canyon.

On Wednesday, a human chain was formed with men spaced about one hundred feet apart, a line that stretched from Timberline Lodge up the mountain past Lone Fir. Starting east of the lodge, they carefully scanned the mountainside, moving west. They soon found Gueffroy's skis standing in the snow between Sand Canyon and Little Zigzag Canyon. The line was then redeployed to search down the slope, but the lateness of the day halted operations. As they trooped toward the Timberline Lodge that night, someone noticed a pattern in the new fallen snow, a series of dimples that were visible only in the oblique rays of sunset. Using a ski pole as a probe, they discovered that, under the dimples, the crust, buried eighteen inches under the new snow, had been broken.

Digging down, they found tracks. The next morning, searchers returned early to probe the slopes with inverted ski poles. On detecting the broken crust, they cleared away the snow with shovels. A course was established that took them down into Sand Canyon. Russ McJury saw Gueffroy's ski pole, and then his pack. One wrist strap had been broken. When they found Gueffroy, they deduced from his position on the crusted base that he sat down for his fatal sleep not much later than 4:30 P.M. on Sunday, the time when the blizzard closed in.

Gueffroy had been known as somewhat of a loner, often skiing away from his group unannounced to cross a ridge or traverse a forest. Trip-mates were accustomed to waiting for him to arrive late, but he knew the terrain and was a capable skier.

There was some criticism of the leadership of Wood and Leuthold in allowing the party to become segmented, especially by Otto Lang, the ski instructor at Timberline Lodge. This was picked up by a *Time* magazine reporter and included in an article in the April 11 edition. However, a full review of the situation resulted in the general opinion that their decisions actually saved lives. If the full party had been held together to come all the way down with Varney, there would probably have been others who would have perished from hypothermia.

It is apparent that the clothing of that era was not as effective as that of today. Winter climbing parties now are expected to be much better clothed and equipped. Even so, Varney was remiss in climbing with inadequate clothing (even for the time period) and in venturing onto the mountain while recuperating from illness. In doing so, he exposed the rest of the party to additional hazard.

One of the disturbing facets of the Varney-Gueffroy incident was that a party member had assured Leuthold and Wood on Sunday night that all members of the party had been accounted for.

It is apparent that the organization of this search mission was in some disarray. There were many agencies involved, but no clearly defined leader responsible for the overall operation. Results like this led to the conclusion that a centralized authority was necessary for search-and-rescue missions. A local government agency dealing with emergencies in the mountains would be the logical choice to assume this role.

Gerald Herrmann Dies of Exposure, 1940

At 1:45 A.M. on Sunday, March 31, 1940, Gerald "Spike" Herrmann, 28, of Milwaukie, Oregon, and James "Jay" Lorentz, 19, of Oregon City, left Timberline Lodge for a summit climb. They did not check in with a ranger that night, so District Forester Harold Engles ordered a search to begin on Monday morning. Volunteers from the Hood River Crag Rats were included in the call-out.

Marshall Stenerson and Joe Leuthold of the Forest Service and Ralph Wiese of the Mount Hood Ski Patrol, along with Ralph Calkin, Herbert Rasor, James Simmons, William Wood, Andy Anderson, and Glen Asher, divided into two groups to search above the ski lift. Harold Engles, Al Haroun, Ralph Hadfield, Dean Stapleton, E.P. McKeen-Smith, Willis Caldwell, and Jack Brotherton skied west to probe in the Little Zigzag Canyon area. Barry James, Paul Livingston, and Ed Meyer hiked to White River Canyon. Meanwhile, a foghorn at the Lodge, and a one thousand-watt searchlight at Silcox Hut were used in the hopes of signaling the lost climbers.

Harold Engles led a climbing party to the summit. The lost pair had been there and entered this note in the summit register: "too cold to write." From this, Engles surmised that they had stumbled off the north side, but the Crag Rats could find no trace of them there. On Monday night, the barometer showed a new storm approaching.

On Tuesday, Ralph Wiese led Horace Mecklem Jr., William Hackett, Chester Wilde, and Thomas Hill on a ski trip around the east side to Cooper Spur. They crossed White River and contoured across the Newton Clark Glacier at the 9,500-foot level. They then returned to Timberline Lodge at 4:00 P.M., having seen no trace of the climbers.

But two others, Jack Nelson and John Pfeiffer, returned in the afternoon from the Zigzag Canyon area with the news that their party had found tracks and intended to follow them, even if it meant staying out all night. Ole Lien was leading the group, which consisted of Ralph Hadfield, Steward Mockford, and William Lanahan. In Paradise Park, at 2:30 A.M., Lanahan came upon Jay Lorentz, who collapsed as his rescuer came into sight. He was dazed, snow-blind, and suffering from hypothermia. Once the two of them reached the Paradise shelter, Lorentz was given food and warmed as much as possible. Hadfield and Mockford were sent at once to the search headquarters at Timberline Lodge to tell the search managers that Lorentz had been found. Lorentz was then taken down the trail to Twin Bridges Campground for further treatment and transportation.

Lorentz told searchers that he had left Herrmann, who was too tired to go further, below Crater Rock. He shielded his friend from the wind as well as he could, with snowshoes and both their packs, and then started down for help. Apparently, probably suffering from hypothermia, Herrmann later started down, too. Both climbers made the common mistake of drifting too far west in low visibility. Russ McJury and Joe Leuthold finally saw Herrmann's body from below through his field glasses. He was lying near the east side of Mississippi Head, frozen, with his head and hands bare.

This is another case of climbers heading up into the summit area in extremely cold weather with inadequate clothing and equipment, and then becoming separated. No details were given regarding the recovery of the body and its return to the Herrmann family.

Helen Lowry, 1943

On Monday, September 6, 1943, Lu Norene, his wife Margaret, Randall Kester, and Portland librarian Helen Lowry decided to climb the Cooper Spur Route from Tilly Jane Camp. It was not a Mazamas climb, even though Norene was chairman of the group's Climbing Committee, and the other three were committee members. It had been the custom for citizens to help man the Forest Service guard stations, as some of the group had been doing that weekend under the direction of guard Alfred T. Maas.

On the descent of the Cooper Spur Route, Miss Lowry slipped and made the two thousand-foot slide down the slope to the Eliot Glacier that so many climbers have experienced. Tragically, in this instance, it resulted in her death. Helping with the evacuation, in addition to members of the climbing party, were Alfred Maas and Boyd French, the operator of Cloud Cap Inn.

This is another example of an "ad-hoc" evacuation being performed by those living and working in the area. Citizen volunteers were becoming more active in the mountains. But there was still no formal organization to conduct searches or rescues, and little coordination between the responders.

The Author's Personal Memories of Mount Hood

This tragedy on the Cooper Spur Route brings back memories of my own experience on the route in late June of 1939. As trail-hiking neophytes from the Hollywood Hills of Southern California, my brother K and I arrived at Cloud Cap Inn with two Los Angeles friends, all with ambitions to tackle the mountain's most treacherous slope. We were greeted with skepticism by the Inn caretaker, who noted our homemade ice axes and smooth-soled, knee-length boots. We were immediately advised not to make the attempt until after the Fourth of July, when the American Legion performed their annual task of installing a rope anchor from the summit down the steep upper part of the route.

After a little discussion, we decided to at least explore the lower part of the route. In the morning, we climbed steadily to the timberline, then up the long barren rocky crest of the lower Cooper Spur. We strapped on our six-point crampons, but, still in our exploring-only mood, we left our fifty-foot rope behind, as we weren't yet acquainted with proper roping-up and belaying techniques.

We then struck out on the hard snow, with all six points of our crampons sinking in firmly. The slope steepened, but only gradually, so we kept exploring until the slope attained an angle of about forty-five degrees. The summit high above appeared to be leaning over us. Slowly, but steadily, we gained elevation, taking a few photos to show the steepness of the slope. After what seemed like an hour, we approached the first of several rock-lined gullies, a few hundred feet below the top.

Several times during the climb, small rocks loosened from sun-warmed snow had come bounding down the slope, skipping and whirring through the air past us. This made us appreciate the precarious nature of our position, and we hastened upward. I gained a small rock platform upon which

"K" Molenaar and Ken Spangenberg on Mount Hood in 1939.   Photo by the author

"K" Molenaar in the old fire lookout, summit of Mount Hood in 1938.   Photo by the author

I had expected to rest comfortably, but I found that the rock sloped downward almost as much as the snow slope. After a little maneuvering, I got into a position where I could watch the others.

Our friend Kenny had found a place above me, and George had worked his way over to the south of the gully and was lying back resting. Then, while maneuvering toward another rock platform, K suddenly lost his footing when his crampon hit some ice beneath the snow. We yelled at him to grab something, but he slid down the slope on his back. We watched in helpless fright as he headed down the slope toward the vertical ice wall and bergschrund on the Eliot Glacier far below.

But K's time had not yet come. His slide was abruptly stopped about fifty feet below, when he hit some soft snow beside the last boulder on the slope. After regaining our composure and glancing warily up and down the slope from our unstable perches, we all felt committed to continue upward rather than trying to descend the slope. After Kenny carefully kicked steps in the softening snow, we followed in each of his steps until the top came upon us. We had a good view along the summit ridge and down the steep slopes on each side. After glancing again, somewhat fearfully, down the steep face up which we had just come, we descended the south slope to Timberline Lodge instead, and hitched a ride back to Cloud Cap.

This close call on Mount Hood demonstrated how much we had to learn before we were ready to climb Northwest volcanoes. We understood very clearly just how close we each had come to being a statistic.

CHAPTER 6

Mountain Rescue Missions in Oregon: 1926–1959

In respect to equipment, we would like to emphasize that the equipment is only as good as the knowledge of the person using it.

THE AMERICAN ALPINE CLUB (1954)

The following accidents occurred soon after formation of the first mountain rescue units in Oregon. Primary sources for these incidents are materials in books by Jack Grauer (1996) and Ric Conrad (2003), and used with their permission.

Vanda York, 1926

On Friday, September 10, 1926, Vanda M. York, from Portland, arrived in Hood River with the intent of hiking to Government Camp. She reached Parkdale that night, and arrived at Cooper Spur Junction on Saturday morning. Curiosity caused her to take a side trip to J. O. Hannum's Homestead Inn, where the conversation tempted her to make an attempt to summit Mount Hood. The Hannums discouraged her, telling her that she was not properly outfitted, but she met Mark Weygandt later in the day, and he offered to guide her to the summit.

Herbert Gordon, a young man working at Tilly Jane Camp, joined Vanda and Mark, and on Sunday morning the three ascended the Eliot Glacier on the way to the Sunshine Route. They had no rope, but decided to climb the last steep area to the slopes above the Langille Crags anyway. When Weygandt stopped to chop steps with his ice ax, Miss York apparently looked north to admire the scenery and somehow slipped. Both Gordon and Weygandt attempted to stop her, but she stumbled across the lower lip of the crevasse, then slipped and fell another sixty feet into the chasm, where she became tightly wedged between the narrowing walls.

Weygandt raced toward a rope cache on the route and quickly brought a coil back to the scene. He tied a loop in the end and dropped it to Miss York. She was able to run it under her arms. Gordon and Weygandt pulled with all their strength, but the girl was too tightly wedged to be moved. Weygandt knew that he must descend and cut her free. As he was considering the problem, he saw a party of climbers descending Cooper Spur. His shouts seemed to have no effect. He was not aware that they had heard him and decided to hurry down for help.

After instructing Gordon on the handling of the rope, Weygandt climbed down into the crevasse on belay, hoping that the inexperienced 140-pound boy would be able to hold him. Before he could reach the girl, however, the crevasse became too narrow for him, and he was forced to chop his way through the ice to get to her. This narrowness also severely impaired his ability to strike effective blows at the ice. Because of hypothermia, Miss York was already unconscious and breathing shallowly. He soon got close enough to throw his coat over her to protect her from the falling ice chips.

Chopping around her body was especially difficult, but when he saw her form sag toward him, he knew she was at last free. He then signaled to Gordon for a belay and climbed back to the surface of the glacier, chopping steps here and there to stem up the walls of ice. He and Gordon then attempted to raise her up to their position. It was a very difficult lift. Once she was up, they wrapped her in coats and eventually succeeded in bringing her back to consciousness. Finally, they got her onto her feet, and began walking her slowly down the Eliot Glacier.

Meanwhile, the group descending Cooper Spur had brought word to Homestead Inn of the problem. Hood River Crag Rats members Kent Shoemaker, A.L. Anderson, Harold Davis, and C.V. Jackson were at work brushing out the new ski hill. They left immediately for Cloud Cap Inn with a timber axe, stove poker, first aid kit, rope, splints, and hot coffee. A call to Don Lamson in Hood River alerted the rest of the Crag Rats organization. By the time the four reached the glacier, Weygandt and Gordon had walked Miss York down to the edge of the moraine. The Crag Rats then took over. Anderson gave her wool socks, warm shoes, and a massage to increase her circulation.

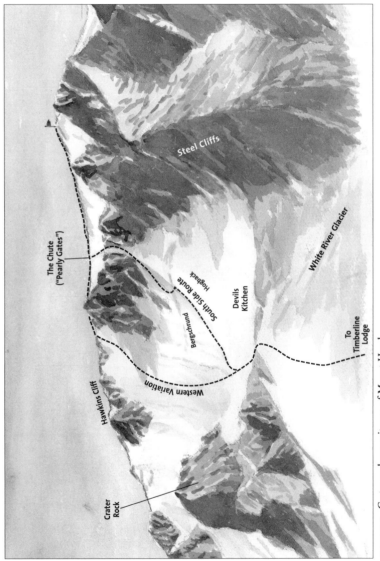

FIGURE 5. Crater and summit area of Mount Hood.

By the time they reached Cloud Cap Inn, Lamson had arrived from Hood River with more than twenty Crag Rats. They took her to Homestead Inn in an automobile. Happily, Miss York had no serious injuries, only swollen hands and feet. On Tuesday, Weygandt drove her to Parkdale, where she could catch the train to Hood River. Miss York indicated that she was determined to return the following year and complete the climb.

This incident shows that the Hood River Crag Rats changed the landscape for search-and-rescue operations soon after the group was founded in 1926. A highly experienced group was available to respond to the emergency, and this would lead to the creation of similar organizations in the Northwest in the late 1940s.

Donald Welk, 1949

On Saturday, October 29, 1949, at about midnight, Donald Welk, 20, his sister Alice, 17, and Robert Buscho, 24, began a climb of Mount Hood's South Side Route. Before sunrise, they had ascended on hard, icy snow to a point within three hundred feet of the summit of Mount Hood. There, Donald Welk slipped, trying in vain to arrest his fall with his alpenstock. He quickly picked up speed in the Chute (a steep trough in a snow gully leading to the summit), tumbling and cartwheeling, as his sister and Buscho helplessly watched him eventually slide out of sight. His slide took him west past Crater Rock, until he finally came to rest in a depression below Illumination Rock.

Buscho started down at once, but by the time he reached the depression, Welk's body was still and cold. Buscho returned to Alice and escorted her down to the top of the ski lift, which, unfortunately, was not yet running at that time of day. A mile of trotting brought him down to Timberline Lodge by 7:30 A.M.

To retrieve Welk's remains, Lift Supervisor James Carskadon assembled a crew of Timberline Lodge employees, including Walter Aeppli, Ben Lintell, and Lewis Byrne, along with Mel Hardy of the Forest Service. As with the early missions on Mount Rainier, these first missions on Mount Hood were ad-hoc assemblies of local climbers and citizens with varying degrees of skill. The party reached Welk's body by 11:30 A.M. and strapped him to a makeshift toboggan constructed from a stretcher and several skis. Their progress across the icy snow was very slow at first, but by 2:00 P.M. they had returned to Timberline Lodge.

Donald Welk had served nineteen months in the U.S. Marine Corps, and was a student at Lewis and Clark College. Alice Welk and Robert Buscho were members of the Mazamas. No one in the group was highly experienced in mountaineering. Inexperience, and the alpenstock failing to stop Welk's slide, were among the causes of this fatal accident.

Lynn Kaufman, 1956

On Sunday, July 29, Carl Schnoor, 20, a college student from Portland, led a group of nineteen teenagers from the east coast up Mount Hood's South Side Route. Schnoor had previously led several such climbs. Unfortunately for the teenagers, however, he tied all of them, closely spaced together, into only one rope, which was generally considered a very poor practice by mountaineers. Descending a chute at 3:45 P.M., they slipped. Schnoor tried, unsuccessfully, to arrest the fall with his ice ax. Only one or two in the group knew how to react to this situation, and that wasn't enough. They quickly picked up speed, until the slide ended in a cleft at the bottom of the slope.

A high school group from Salem, consisting of Thomas and Louise Pfau, Dennis Glasgow, Frank Franklin, and Gail Wright witnessed the accident. They quickly carried the news to the Timberline Lodge snowcat driver on Palmer Glacier, who relayed it to personnel at the lodge. The Forest Service and lodge personnel promptly went to work. A phone call brought Dr. Elton Leavitt and his partner, Dr. William Rohrberg, up the mountain to help. Timberline Lodge equipment operator Richard Kohnstamm became the lead snowcat operator for the rescue. Ralph Wiese and James Langdon of the Forest Service took what other help they could get and headed for the crater.

At 6:00 P.M., after an ascent of North Sister in central Oregon, John Biewener of the Mountain Rescue and Safety Council of Oregon and his friend, Dr. James Owen, were having dinner at the Tramway House restaurant in Government Camp. Once told of the accident, they hurried to the scene. By that time, however, Doctors Leavitt and Rohrberg were already examining the dozen victims who had been laid out on the Hogsback by Forest Service and Timberline Lodge personnel. Six of the victims had already been sent out under their own power.

Biewener consoled some of the victims by telling them: "In thirty minutes, you are going to see a solid stream of lights down there on the road." Sure enough, within half an hour, MRSCO members began to crowd the highway from Portland and Hood River, lighting up the timbered slopes below.

The Air Force sent ambulances, doctors, and medical corpsmen, and also dropped blood plasma and drugs from one of their aircraft. To check the victims, they set up a medical battle station at the top of the ski lift at Silcox Hut. The Coast Guard sent helicopters. The two services contributed four aircraft and more than twenty-five rescuers to the operation. Eighty blankets were stripped from the beds at Timberline Lodge. Everett Darr opened his Mountain Shop at Government Camp and told the rescuers: "Take what you need."

By 11:00 P.M., ninety Mountain Rescue and Safety Council of Oregon team members had arrived at the crater with stretchers, akias (rescue sleds), radios, and lights. Thirteen stretchers were carried down that night, the last containing the body of the only victim who did not survive her injuries, Lynn Kaufman. On Palmer Glacier, the bobbing flashlights and the lights of the snowcat presented a surreal scene to those watching from below. By 3:15 A.M., all the stretchers had been brought to the Air Force battle station at the Silcox Hut.

Once the victims arrived there, Timberline Lodge became an emergency hospital. Doctors and nurses worked throughout the night. By morning, sixteen patients had been moved to Emanuel, Providence, and Good Samaritan hospitals in Portland.

The casualties included Lynn Kaufman, deceased; Judith Harth, an injured back and broken ankle; Lawrence D. McCormick, a broken hand; Diesel O. Shaw, a broken leg and injured arm; Patricia Shaw, lacerations; Suzanne Blum, a broken back and brain concussion; John Schloss, a leg injury; Barbara Platto, two broken legs; Robert H. Silin, a cut leg; Susan Stein, a fractured skull; Ronal Heinrich, a broken shoulder; Claire E. Mitchell, two broken ankles; and Sidney H. Rosenberg, an injured leg.

David Draper, 1959

On Saturday, June 20, 1959, at about 1:00 P.M., a climbing party of forty Boy Scouts and two leaders started their descent from the summit of

Mount Hood via the South Side Route. The leaders, Amos Smelser and John McClosky, were part of the last rope team to leave the summit. Just ahead of them was a roped team consisting of Edward W. Smith, 47, and Don Berger, 38, along with three scouts, David Draper, 15; William Halling, 16; and Thomas McCune, 14.

About two hundred feet below the summit, Smelser noticed a stream of slushy snow pouring off the rocks above. It was about eighteen inches deep and forty feet wide. "Anchor in!" he yelled. Berger was able to get a good hold with his ice ax, but the heavy stream hit Smith and the three boys, carrying them downhill. Berger could not hold the fall, so all five were swept to the bottom of a crevasse below.

Smelser and McClosky moved quickly to the crevasse to help. But, within minutes, the slush had hardened into ice, trapping the victims in various positions. One of the boys was only ankle-deep, and one of the men was immersed to his waist. The other three were almost completely covered, with David Draper lying on the bottom. While Smelser worked feverishly to chop them free, word was sent below for help. A Mountain Rescue and Safety Council of Oregon team, led by Keith Petrie, assembled to make the evacuation.

When the group leaders reached Draper, he was blue, and not breathing. To complicate matters further, the slush continued to intermittently flow into the accident site. It froze quickly, and began filling the crevasse. By the time the last victims were removed, so much had poured down that the rescuers were able to climb out of the crevasse on the frozen slush without any direct lifting with climbing ropes.

The leaders attempted to revive Draper for about four hours, but he never regained consciousness. Smith was able to help himself out of the crevasse after being chopped free of the ice. All of the victims were then loaded into a snowcat for the trip down to Timberline Lodge. All but Berger were then sent to the hospital.

By 1959, mountain rescue in the Pacific Northwest had become better organized. Just before this incident, many teams in Oregon and Washington had banded together to form the national Mountain Rescue Association. See the final chapter of this book for more details on the MRA.

CHAPTER 7

Multi-Unit Mount McKinley Mission, 1960

*Another warning, hardly less distinctly
uttered and hardly less important, is against
the slackened rope, the best friend of the
climber converted only too easily to his most
insidious and dangerous foe.*

SIR ALFRED WILLS (1867)

In 1959, the Mountain Rescue Association (MRA) was established as the first national mountain rescue organization in the United States. This set the stage for a regional response in Alaska that would test the effectiveness of this new concept.

The Call-Out

For me, it started with a phone call from Ralph Johnson of the Seattle Mountain Rescue Council at 11:00 P.M. on May 17, 1960, requesting that I get my gear together for a flight to Alaska to help rescue some friends who had fallen on Mount McKinley (also known as Denali). This was to be the most massive mountain-rescue operation staged in American mountaineering history up to that time.

The accident occurred on the West Buttress Route, where John Day, an affluent Oregon rancher, had decided to test his forty-eight-year-old body against the mountain. He made the climb with the help of Jim and Lou Whittaker, Seattle's energetic climbing twins with whom he had been setting speed records on several volcanoes in Oregon and Washington. To round out the party, they enlisted the help of Pete Schoening, a legend in his own time for his famed ice-ax anchor during the 1953 American K2 expedition, a belaying feat that saved six lives, including my own.

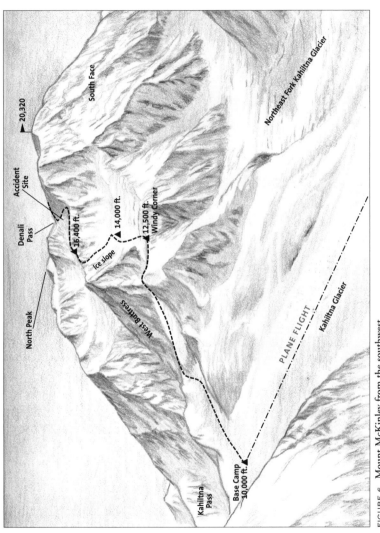

FIGURE 6. Mount McKinley from the southwest.

Jim and Lou Whittaker with Hans Fuhrer in 1951.   Photo by the author

Instead of the usual Park Service-approved landing site on the Kahiltna Glacier at 7,500 feet, the Day party received special permission to land on the glacier at 10,000 feet, ostensibly for the purpose of researching and recording snow and glacier conditions. This head start apparently allowed this party to reach the summit in only three days. On the mountain at the same time were an Anchorage party led by Paul Crews, and two parties representing different Japanese universities.

The Day Party followed the Crews Party to the summit, where they were both duly photographed in fine weather. However, because of a slip during their descent down the ice slope below Denali Pass, the Day group suffered an accident that left some of its members injured seriously enough to require evacuation. Fortunately for them, the Crews party, some distance below, witnessed the fall and, with their radio, were able to send out a call for help. Crews descended to the Day camp and brought back their tent, which he placed over John Day, who had suffered two broken ankles. The Whittakers were slightly groggy, but otherwise uninjured. Schoening, however, had frostbitten fingers.

The call for help resulted in the rapid notification of mountain rescue units from Anchorage, Fairbanks, Seattle, Tacoma, Everett, Bremerton, and Portland. A dozen Puget Sound area climbers with high-altitude experience and equipment were immediately enlisted to form the first group heading for Alaska. Besides me, this advance party included

George Senner, Gene Prater, Gary Rose, Dr. Otto Trott, Dick Wahlstrom, Paul Gerstmann, Walt Gonnason and Steve Anderson. All of these individuals had experience on Mount Rainier. With only a couple of hours notice, we had to gather our gear and clothing and meet at the SeaTac airport by 1:00 A.M. Eventually, more than sixty mountain-rescue personnel would respond. In fact, it was conjectured that, thanks to John Day's financial largesse, anyone wandering near the airport with an ice ax and pack could have obtained a free flight to Anchorage.

On May 18, the Air Force flew us to a place near the town of Summit, on the flatlands east of Mount McKinley. According to the reports coming in from the mountain, there were at least four and possibly five stretcher cases awaiting evacuation. This number included Helga Bading of Paul Crews' party, who was suffering pulmonary edema at their 16,500-foot camp.

Contemplating the evacuation of this many people down the steep slopes of McKinley, possibly under deteriorating weather conditions, made many of us regret we hadn't started climbing earlier in the year to get into better shape. But several of the others were in good shape as a result of planning forthcoming expeditions to McKinley in June and to Mount McArthur in the St. Elias Mountains that summer. In fact, we owed our food supply during this effort to the generous response of the members of these two parties, who turned over their prepared supplies to the rescue effort—in effect canceling their own expeditions.

Cold-weather clothing had to be taken unceremoniously and in great quantity from Seattle-based equipment store REI. This was to be a post-rescue headache for REI manager and accident victim Jim Whittaker. A "banana" chopper dropped us at a sand bar at the confluence of a couple of large channels of the Kahiltna River. We were still on the flatlands of Alaska, but were now within sight of McKinley, which rises beyond the foothill peaks. The chopper left in a blast of sand that had us scurrying around to protect our loose gear. We were not given an assignment, so we pitched our tents for the night.

At dusk, George Senner and I were about to catch up on some sleep when three ski-equipped airplanes landed next to camp. An authoritative voice from a person carrying a clipboard requested that Prater, Senner and I immediately collect our gear and board these aircraft. Half asleep, we were hustled out of our tents by numerous hands, and, with hastily packed gear, we found ourselves each assigned to one of the planes. Upon hearing Don Sheldon advising the other two pilots on how to make a landing on the mountain, Prater quickly jumped into Sheldon's plane, while George and I climbed aboard the other two. With blasts of sand, we were finally in the air and heading for the mountain.

On Denali

For sixty miles, we flew over an increasingly spectacular and rugged landscape of ice and rock. As we approached the upper Kahiltna Glacier, we saw far below the brilliantly colored camp of the two Japanese expeditions. All fifteen climbers from these expeditions had reached the summit and returned to their camp, and were now waiting for Sheldon to carry them back to Talkeetna. After circling a few times, my plane followed Sheldon's in for a soft landing on the snow. The plane got slightly stuck, and I had to get out and push. It was quite a chore to suddenly have to exert myself at 10,000 feet.

After all three planes had safely landed and then taken off with three of the Japanese climbers for the return to Talkeetna, we were invited by the remaining Japanese climbers to have tea and rice with them in their communal tent. Our arrival had given them their first news of the accident. They kindly invited us to use one of their spacious tents for the night. The night was clear, cold (about 10 degrees below zero Fahrenheit), and short, with dawn coming only a couple of hours after darkness during the early summer at this latitude.

In the morning, a large "banana" chopper and more ski planes delivered additional climbers. After a brief consultation, nine of us prepared for the climb to the 14,000-foot level, which was hidden beyond the south shoulder of the West Buttress. The climb to 14,000 feet

Rescuers on approach at 11,000 feet on Denali, 1960.   Photo by the author

started out comfortably enough, as our route was initially in shadow, but, as the sun rounded the mountain and hit us directly, our cold-weather clothing quickly became superfluous. However, the snowshoes provided to us by the Army were definitely needed as we trudged upward.

After reaching hard ice lying beneath three to four inches of powder snow at 11,000 feet, we cached the snowshoes. Above 12,000-foot Windy Corner lay a broad plateau-cirque that consumed much of our energy. By evening, Gene Prater, George Senner, Walt Gonnason, Gary Rose, Dick Wahlstrom and I reached the vast 14,000-foot basin below the upper West Buttress. During the day, several large parachute drops had been made by a cargo plane flying about 2,000 feet above our basin. Air-dropped tents were eventually pitched, and stoves topped with soup and other warm, comforting liquids soon helped us forget the hardships of the day's trek; food had little appeal to me. From here, we had our first view of the upper West Buttress. It merged into a ridge that extended above the basin and to the southwest face of the South Peak, the summit of which was out of sight along the upper right skyline. The ice slopes descending from the West Buttress to the left created some misgivings; it would not be easy to lower injured men down the long forty-degree expanses of blue ice without a slip. My sleep that night was beset by much apprehension.

Meanwhile, chopper pilot Link Luckett had just done the impossible; he had picked up John Day at 17,000 feet. Day was now safely in an Anchorage hospital. Helga Bading, of the Anchorage party, was brought down to the 14,000-foot level by Paul Crews and Chuck Metsger in an air-dropped akia sled. She was then flown out by Don Sheldon, who had landed his ski-equipped plane in a basin just below.

We also received news that a small plane with two people aboard had crashed and burned at the 17,000-foot level, near the high camp of the Seattle party. But, contrary to what the newspapers initially reported, the plane was not part of the rescue or air-drop operations. In fact, the pilot had been told to keep away from the mountain. According to Schoening and the Whittakers, the plane had come too close to the cliffs. When the pilot attempted to turn away, he banked too steeply and lost lift. When he increased power to come out of the resultant dive, the aircraft continued straight into the mountain.

On May 20, we were awakened early by a helicopter circling high over the ridge above. Luckett had returned and was now evacuating Pete

Schoening. We all felt better when Paul Crews gave us the good news that the Whittakers were in good enough shape to climb down on their own if a helicopter wasn't available. Unfortunately, clouds were increasing, and the weather in the summit area was rapidly deteriorating. But even so, it was time to move up and help the Whittakers descend.

The Rescue

I roped up with Metsger and Crews who, being well acclimatized, carried my pack. We started across the basin and toward the base of the ice slope, with Senner, Gary Rose, and Gene Prater following on a second rope. As we climbed to 15,000 feet, my breathing became labored, but I felt no other ill effects as we ascended the fixed rope left by the Japanese climbers to the rocky ridge crest. Moving slightly ahead of the Senner party, we continued to the right up the ridge crest to the 16,400-foot camp of the Anchorage party. The Whittakers had arrived there from their higher camp earlier. I could hear them laughing inside their tent as I approached with the query, "Is the Co-op open?"

Lou's neck was slightly sprained, to the extent that any sudden movement made him feel unsteady on his legs. So he left his pack, which was later brought down by the Anchorage climbers when they evacuated their camp a day or two later. I roped up with Jim and Lou. I was tied in the middle, belaying them below me on a doubled rope. We descended to the col (a gap between peaks) above the ice slope, where Senner, Rose and Prater helped us by carrying part of our heavy loads as we carefully worked our way down the fixed rope to the lower slope. Our arrival at 14,000 feet was greeted with loud cheers by the Whittakers' friends.

After a little more liquid, we again roped up, aiming to reach the 10,000-foot base camp that evening. But the weather was still changing for the worse. It was beginning to snow and blow. The willow-wand trail helped us, but by the time we arrived at 13,000-foot Windy Corner, we were in a full-scale blizzard. Soft snow had drifted deeply into the hollows, which caused us to flounder as we sought to stay on the route. Then, a few shouts from below through the mists disclosed another party at Windy Corner. Dr. Otto Trott, upon learning that the Whittakers were all right, was exuberant in his greetings. As they already had a camp a short distance below, and because of the storm, we decided to camp with them.

Storm at 13,000 feet during 1960 Mount McKinley Rescue.   Photo by the author

Stuck in the Tents

Soon ropes and crampons were off, and we crawled inside the Army hexagonal tent to be greeted by others. The comfort inside that tent, and the camaraderie, made us forget all about descending further. The wind was pulling at the tent fabric and telling us to settle down here for the night. But if we had known what was in store for us the next day and following night, we might have continued down to base camp instead.

Later in the evening, a few of us moved into four small tents which had been pitched nearby. Senner and I joined Charles "Bucky" Wilson in his tent, where, although the tent pressed in on us, we felt quite secure from the storm. Cozy inside our sleeping-bag cocoons, we accepted this retreat from all concerns, but dozed fitfully throughout the night.

During that night of May 21, the storm increased in fury, and by morning, most of the small tents had either been torn or blown down. By noon, all but Paul Gerstmann had deserted the small tents and were now sitting or lying spoke-fashion inside the five-man Army tent, trying to hold the tent down. Paul decided that he was still quite cozy in his sleeping bag in one of the downed tents, so he hibernated beneath his flapping nylon cover.

The day and night spent in the big tent will long remain in all of our memories. The Whittakers lay stretched against the tent wall. They were quite conversant about the accident, and many questions were thrown at them between the noisy periods of whipping wind. The tent flapped and crackled almost continually, although occasionally we imagined the wind was abating. I remember sharing much of the time with Gene Prater and Vic Josendal while lending support to the tent's creaking center pole.

Two small stoves, handled efficiently by Otto Trott, were on at all times, except when carelessly knocked over by a foot or elbow. Warm food and hot liquids were always welcome. Entering and leaving the tent through the zippered inner and outer linings was an operation in itself. Eventually, as the fabric adjacent to the zipper lining began ripping, we tried to curtail the number of such enterings and leavings. But mother nature couldn't be denied, and sooner or later all of us had to experience some uncomfortable time outside the tent. Yet some occupants remained hidden deep within sleeping bags and were rarely heard from except for their grunts when tea or soup was passed around. A few years later, I was still meeting fellows who claim they were in that tent, which suggests there must have been fifteen to twenty people in that five-man tent.

The storm gradually eased off on Monday morning (May 22). The tent looked like it wouldn't hold for another hour, so we prepared to leave the scene. Crampons and ice axes had to be located in the deep

Descent at 11,000 feet during 1960 Mount McKinley Rescue. From left: George Senner, Gene Prater, Lou Whittaker, and Jim Whittaker.   Photo by the author

drifts around the tent, and packs rearranged, before we finally roped up and headed down into the still-swirling fog. But, amazingly, and in no time at all, two of our rope teams, including the Whittakers, Senner, Prater, Gonnason, and I, had descended below the wind-blasted slopes and were in a zone of deep, drifting snow. There we put on our previously cached snowshoes and continued in gradually clearing weather. Our orientation was somewhat off, however, and it was with great surprise that we suddenly found ourselves in base camp at 10,000 feet, earlier than we had expected to get there. We were all welcomed with hot tea, soup, and food.

Base Camp

Comfortably ensconced in base camp, which included several large Logan tents and Army hexagonals, was a large group that included such notables as Fred Beckey, Don Claunch, Ed Cooper, Barry Corbet, Max Eckenburg, Jon Garde, Bob Grant, Keith Hart, Al Krup, Everett Lasher, Jim Nelson, Jack Newman, and Al Randall. Many were frustrated by not being allowed to move higher and become more involved in the operation. But, in this vast expanse of deep powder snow, we could understand the relief of the wall-climbers in the group.

Finally unroped and free, George and I made a big thing of neatly arranging our packs and bags in a spacious Logan tent, anticipating the possibility of another night or two here before being flown out. As we lay in the luxury of the tent, however, we heard the approach of another group from above, and soon the camp was welcoming rescuers arriving from Windy Corner. But there was still no word from the 14,000-foot camp. Eventually, an unusually clear radio contact informed us that those above had decided to wait out the storm before moving down.

The weather cleared toward evening, and soon a sparkling winter world was revealed. Fresh snow covered the ridges and ramparts of the West Buttress above. The clearing continued to the south down the glacier. We thought that Don Sheldon's ski plane would soon appear, checking on landing possibilities for the "banana" choppers. Sure enough, no sooner had Senner and I repacked our gear and rolled up our sleeping bags than we heard the faint chop-chop of a helicopter, along with the whir of Sheldon's plane, which circled and then landed at the edge of camp.

When Sheldon came out of the plane and spotted the Whittakers running toward him, he let out a whoop and, minus snowshoes, made long leaping strides toward camp. Sheldon and the Whittakers met with a big three-man bear hug. It was evident that Sheldon felt strongly toward these two boys he had deposited at this camp more than a week before. Then a "banana" chopper came in, kicking up the usual snowstorm. As soon as it stopped, it discharged three more men, and then, almost immediately, the Whittakers, Senner, Prater, Steve Johnson, and I loaded up and headed for the aircraft. Lou got in with Sheldon, and the rest of us boarded the chopper. Then we were off, finally free of the mountain's snowy grip.

In Anchorage, the Whittakers were greeted by their wives amidst the crackling of the flashbulbs of dozens of news photographers. The rest of us gathered our gear together and hopped into waiting taxis for the short journey to the Air Force barracks at nearby Richardson Field, where we were to be quartered for the night. Although near midnight, it was not completely dark, and, after a hearty midnight breakfast, we spent a couple of hours driving around Anchorage seeking out personal equipment that had been left behind when we went to the mountain. At 3:00 A.M., we finally hit the sack.

By Tuesday, May 23, the Whittakers had been checked over at the hospital and found to be in excellent shape. John Day was still in the local hospital, but Pete Schoening had already left for Seattle, where he was hospitalized for frostbitten fingers. He eventually lost the first joints of the fingers on his left hand.

Return to Seattle

A few of us caught the afternoon flight from Anchorage to Seattle, and we enjoyed clear views en route as twilight set in, but many of the other rescue personnel were still on the mountain and had to await a later flight out. As it turned out, the party camped at 14,000 feet had to suffer a few more feet of snowfall for the next several days, and finally had to rely on air-dropped snowshoes for their descent to base camp.

This accident was caused in part by the group's effort to set a speed record; they didn't take adequate time to acclimatize to the mountain's 20,320-foot elevation. Although there was ample manpower recruited for the rescue effort, a communication problem during the operation resulted from the differing radio frequencies in the several rescue units. This made rescuers aware of the need for coordination within the rescue-communications network, and led to the development of common frequencies and better equipment in the following years.

Approximately sixty individuals were involved in this Mount McKinley Rescue:

AERIAL SUPPORT: Men, planes and helicopters from the Army Air Force; Civilian fixed-wing pilots Don Sheldon, Jack Wilson, and George Kitchen; and helicopter pilot Link Luckett (who evacuated Day and Schoening from 17,000 feet).

RESCUE UNITS ON THE MOUNTAIN: Groups from Anchorage, Fairbanks, Seattle, Tacoma, Bremerton, Everett, and Portland.

ACCOMPANIED THE WHITTAKERS DOWN FROM THE 16,400-FOOT RIDGE CREST: Dee Molenaar, George Senner, Gene Prater, and Gary Rose.

SUPPORT AT 14,000-FOOT BASIN: Dr. Paul Gerstmann, Glenn Kelsey, Dick Wahlstrom, Roy Harniss, Johnny Johnson, Walt Gonnason, and Ron Priebe.

SUPPORT AT 13,000-FOOT WINDY CORNER: Dr. Otto Trott, Ty Harkness, Larry Heggerness, Vic Josendal, Paul Williams, and Charles "Bucky" Wilson.

SUPPORT AT 10,000-FOOT BASE CAMP ON UPPER KAHILTNA GLACIER: Max Eckenburg, Al Krup, Everett Lasher, Fred Beckey, Don Claunch, Ed Cooper, Barry Corbet, Keith Hart, Eric Barnes, Marv Fisher, Jon Garde, Bob Godwin, Bob Grant, Jim Messick, Hans Metz, Jim Nelson, Joe Pichler, Norm Pichler, Bill Schlegel, Keith Petrie, and Ross Petrie.

SUPPORT AT TALKEETNA: Ome Daiber, John Simac, Lee Tegner, Harry Conner, Wally Minor, Ed Drues, Jerry Hoyer, John Johnston, Les Robinson, and Scott Wesley.

SUPPORT IN ANCHORAGE: Ralph Johnson, Al Randall, Ray Conkling, Don Jones, Jack Newman, Chuck DeHan, Cecil Hailey, Mark Haun, Bob Leighton, Dave Nelson, and Barry Palmer.

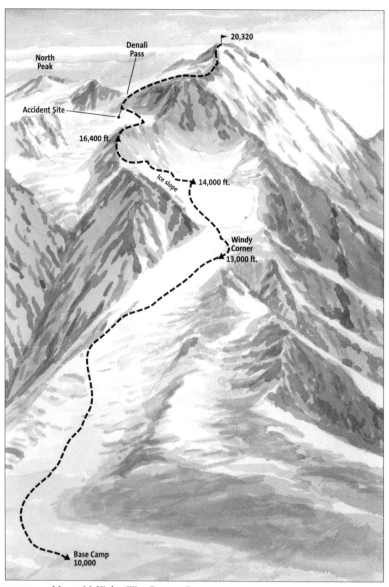

FIGURE 7. Mount McKinley, West Buttress Route.

CHAPTER 8

History of Mountain Rescue Units in Washington

Before a person can be a rescuer, he must first be a climber, completely familiar with mountaineering techniques and equipment.

WOLF BAUER (2008)

The Cascade and Olympic ranges in Washington State attract active outdoors enthusiasts from all over the world. Because of the easy access to the many attractive peaks of these two ranges, this area was destined to become a mountaineering Mecca, but, unfortunately, wherever there are mountains and mountaineers, there will be accidents. Helping the victims of accidents in isolated areas requires individuals with special skills. For maximum efficiency and effectiveness in rescue operations, as many skilled mountaineers as possible must be organized into mountain rescue units.

There were occasional rescue efforts during the early days of climbing in Washington, but, by the 1930s, accidents were so common that more organization became necessary. Lists of experienced climbers were compiled and screened for competence and availability, and telephone committees were formed to call those climbers in the event of an emergency. After the end of World War II, Seattle Mountain Rescue was organized. It was modeled, to some extent, on European rescue teams.

Seattle Mountain Rescue

The following account of Seattle Mountain Rescue's beginnings is primarily from an interview with Wolf Bauer, a leading figure in the organization of the unit.

Climbers in the Pacific Northwest have been rescuing their fellow climbers since the sport began. The well-known tragedy on Mount Rainier in the winter of 1936 that took the life of Delmar Fadden triggered the first steps toward organized rescue outside the National Park Service. Fadden, who yearned to climb in the Himalayas, made an ambitious solo mid-winter ascent of the mountain via the Emmons Glacier Route, but he perished during the descent. Well-known climber Ome Daiber, who had made the first ascent of Liberty Ridge with Arnie Campbell and Will H. (Jim) Borrow, was contacted to help with the search. Ome and several of his friends were involved in the week-long search and the eventual recovery of Fadden's body. This much-publicized recovery created a great demand for Ome whenever there was a need for search or rescue in alpine areas. Over a period of years, Ome developed a list of climbers that he could depend on in an emergency. This informal group conducted a large number of successful operations, some technical in nature, over the next fifteen years.

After World War II, Ome Daiber's fellow Seattle climbers Wolf Bauer, Kurt Beam, and Dr. Otto Trott, all of whom had come to the Northwest from the mountains of Europe in the late 1920s and early 1930s, made periodic visits to their homelands. Returning from one of these visits, Wolf Bauer, who was the founder of the climbing course offered by The Mountaineers of Seattle, called Ome's group together and screened a short movie titled "Bergwacht," which had been produced by the famed Bergwacht rescue team in Innsbruck, Austria.

During a post-screening session, this informal group concluded that climbing in the Northwest had matured sufficiently to require a formal organization to cope with the increasing number of alpine emergencies. Thus was born Seattle Mountain Rescue. Ome's pocket list of names formed the nucleus of the new organization. Many climbers were involved in this effort. Some of the other prominent members were Arnie Campbell, Max Eckenburg, and Dorrell Looff.

The group was officially organized in the spring of 1948 under the sponsorship of The Mountaineers, the Washington Alpine Club, and the Northwest Region of the National Ski Patrol. Originally known as just the Mountain Rescue Council, the team later added "Seattle" to its name, to distinguish itself from other rescue groups that began forming throughout the area, and became known as the Seattle Mountain Rescue Council. Early SMRC members were involved in the formation of some of those teams—they spoke to the founders, encouraged them, and advised them. As a result, some of those other teams initially saw themselves as "subgroups" of the SMRC. Today, the group is called Seattle Mountain Rescue.

In the group's first three or four years, SMRC missions were few, and there was little in the way of organized training. But this soon changed as more veterans and families went to the mountains for recreation. By 1952, the number of accidents and incidents had increased. This made it necessary to formalize the call-out procedures and to institute a regular training program.

An Early Training

An account of a multi-group mountain rescue training was included in the SMRC newsletter's July 1955 edition.

During the weekend of June 11–12, 1955, a two-day rescue training was held at Stevens Pass, in Washington's Cascade Range. It proved to be a great success, with the participation of well over one hundred rescuers from all parts of the Northwest United States, along with some from Colorado and British Columbia.

The main project for Saturday afternoon was an avalanche rescue operation under the direction of Bill Parke of the Forest Service. A dummy was buried in a man-made slide set off by Parke and Frank Foto. A hasty search party, led by Otto Ross of Orondo, Washington, demonstrated the initial actions necessary to locate a slide victim. A follow-up party led by Lou Whittaker performed organized probing, and eventually located the dummy.

While the avalanche search was underway, another group departed for an unknown spot on one of the ridges near Stevens Pass. This group was to be the bivouac party—the object of the next day's search. It was comprised of Cliff Plouff, Arnie Campbell, "victim" Frank Foto, Ed Chalcraft of the *Seattle Post-Intelligencer*, and about six others. Observers from the armed forces also went along.

The Saturday evening program at Summit Inn consisted of the introduction of and short statements by delegates from various coordinating agencies, as well as informal reports by various area groups. Ome Daiber announced that because of professional obligations, he was unable to continue as chairman of the SMRC. The board members present voted to wait until the next board meeting to accept his resignation.

Early Seattle Mountain Rescue Council training at Snoqualmie Pass in Washington's Cascade Range in 1949. Standing, from left: Chuck Welsh, Dee Molenaar, Coast Guard pilot, "K" Molenaar, Max Eckenburg, Ome Daiber, Coast Guard crew member, John Thompson, and Lou Whittaker. Kneeling, from left: Wolf Bauer, unknown rescuer, Jim Whittaker, and Coast Guard pilot.   Photo courtesy of University of Washington Library, Special Collections Division

At 5:00 A.M. on Sunday, a reconnaissance party led by Dr. Otto Trott left Stevens Pass in the general direction of the bivouac party on Big Chief Ridge and signaled their location. The reconnaissance and bivouac parties soon joined up and moved up the ridge, to be subsequently joined by a large group of SMRC members and observers.

The Alpinees, a search-and-rescue group from Hood River, Oregon, demonstrated a skyline cable evacuation of two "victims"—Frank Foto and my wife, Colleen—who were lowered over cliffs in stretchers. The complete rope operation was effected by a team composed of Pete Schoening, Ralph Johnson, William "Bill" Unsoeld (who would later adopt the nickname "Willi"), Ward Irwin, and several other rock experts. A snow-evacuation team led by Kurt Beam operated at the lower levels to get the victims to the highway. All simulated rescues were completed by early afternoon.

A Coast Guard helicopter, piloted by Lieutenant Swanson, participated throughout the practice rescues and evacuations, at elevations up to 5,000 feet. He demonstrated the versatility for which this craft is famous. The helicopter crew landed rescue personnel on the ridge and made a hovering evacuation. They scouted, transported observers and photographers, and demonstrated the use of the helicopter's winch and cable systems for man-lifting.

Perfect weather throughout the weekend contributed to the success of the sessions. A final critique was held Sunday afternoon at Summit Inn. Communications coordination and Civil Air Patrol coordination were the subjects of the greatest amount of discussion. It was evident that the fine cooperative work carried on between SMRC members and the other agencies behind the scenes is one of the most vital of the SMRC's activities.

SMRC was joined in the training session by units from the Coast Guard, Navy, Army, Air Force, U.S. Forest Service, National Park Service, King County Sheriff, Royal Canadian Mounted Police, Civil Air Patrol, and the Washington State Patrol. The success of this combined training was a factor that led to the development of a national mountain rescue organization four years later at Mount Hood.

SMRC: The Early Years

SMRC missions were infrequent during the late 1940s. In 1952 and 1953, however, this team felt the full brunt of the rapidly increasing recreational use of the wilderness. During those two years, more than fifteen full-scale rescues were mounted for a wide variety of incidents: avalanches, lightning strikes, crevasse falls, glissading accidents, falls off cliffs, rappelling accidents, rock fall, and four aircraft crashes. The aircraft accidents alone claimed forty victims. The extensive publicity stemming from these numerous

Dr. Otto Trott and Ome Daiber with a reporter after a rescue mission.

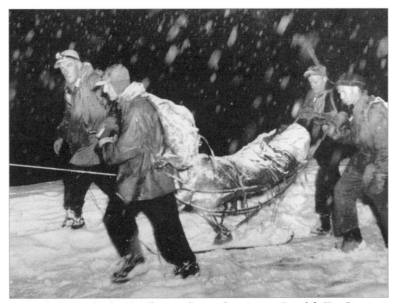

Rescue of Bill Degenhardt with a "bergtrage" rescue litter in 1954. From left: Kurt Beam, Dr. Otto Trott, Al Krup, and Wolf Bauer.   Photo courtesy of The Spring Trust for Trails

missions provided the impetus to better prepare for the future. Meanwhile, additional well-known climbers took active leadership roles in the SMRC, and increased activity provided the foundation for the group's current operation.

Over the next few years, the movement toward organized rescue groups included the formation of Explorer Search and Rescue. In 1959, the national Mountain Rescue Association was formed at Mount Hood, with Dick Pooley of Portland as its first president. By the end of the decade, the MRA included teams in Oregon, Washington, Alaska, Idaho, Montana, Colorado, Arizona, and California. The SMRC logo, originally designed by Wolf Bauer with the help of Dr. Otto Trott, was adopted for use by the MRA, and was copyrighted.

It also became obvious that cooperation from public agencies, such as the U.S. Forest Service, National Park Service, local and state police and sheriff units, as well as any air search-and-rescue group would be absolutely necessary. While members of The Mountaineers wanted to maintain their operations strictly as a public service, paying for expenses out of their own pockets, it was nevertheless important to keep public agencies and the general public aware of needed equipment and operation expenses.

To that end, The Mountaineers took a leading role in establishing and staffing the Seattle Mountain Rescue Council. Dr. Otto Trott of the Mount Baker Ski Patrol became a leader in the organization, tending to its medical needs in the field. It was also natural for Ome Daiber to head many of the missions. Meanwhile, Wolf served as a catalyst for the design and improvement of equipment and field techniques, ran annual conventions and training sessions, and, during the early years, gained governmental input, acceptance, and public support. The SMRC members all profited by creating life-long friendships and gaining the satisfaction of having promoted safe travel habits in the mountains of the Pacific Northwest.

It Was Just Ducky!

Here is an excerpt from the February 6, 1957 SMRC newsletter that describes one of the group's more amusing rescue efforts:

> Frankly, we didn't recognize SMRC Chairman Dorrell Looff when he peered at us from the front page of the February 3 *Seattle Sunday Times*. But then, we are not used to seeing Dorrell with an armful of duck. In case you missed it, SMRC was called on a mission of mercy in south Seattle to rescue a duck that had been trapped in a 90-foot abandoned well. The duck had turned up missing at Thanksgiving and the owners assumed he would never be seen again. However, the duck was heard quacking in a well, so SMRC was called. Dorrell was lowered on a rope manned by Paul Williams, Ray Moore, Frank Taylor and Bill Westbo. The Times quoted Dorrell: "It fought me. The bottom is about 10 feet square and I had to chase it into a corner." The four helpers and Dorrell also got a half-page-wide picture on page 2 of the same edition. Good publicity for SMRC and further proof SMRC is right at home in fowl weather.

Mountain Rescue Communications History: Radios, Call Girls, The FART Team and a Mexican Radio License

The information in this section was written in 2008 by Mike Norman, the first MRA Communications Chairman, now retired.

Mountain rescue operations are held together by communications between personnel in the field, the rescue base, and the in-town coordinator. Additional communications may be required for air support, and with the authorities responsible for responding to the incident. In the early days, at best you were handed a "portable" radio by someone from one of the groups in charge with instructions to call if you needed something or had something to report. Battery drain did not allow you to keep the radio on, so a time was set each hour to turn the radio on, check in, and listen for incoming messages.

The term *portable* could refer to any of several types of radios. In the 1950s, the hand-held portable radios we use today did not exist. The most common portable radio was a Motorola tube-type radio with a handset and a three-foot antenna. This unit weighed about ten pounds with its protective case and batteries. To this, you had to add one or more spare sets of batteries—at five pounds per set—to feed the voracious appetite of the tubes in the radio. These radios were designed to talk back to a law enforcement vehicle at the end of the road. During one operation in Washington, repeated calls from the accident scene to the Washington State Patrol car parked next to the helicopter at the highway went unanswered. After declaring I had "emergency traffic," a weak reply was received, not from the patrol car five miles away, but from a dispatcher with the Michigan state police. After I explained our need, he sent a teletype to our State Patrol headquarters in Olympia, which in turn forwarded it to the North Bend detachment, which in turn radioed the officer stationed with the helicopter and told him to send the chopper in to pick up our victim.

The Forest Service had "portable" radios in plywood cases about the size of two shoe boxes. These put out two watts on HF frequencies, which were much lower than the frequencies used by the handset portables. They came with wire antennas that were about fifty feet long that you could toss into a tree. Operating in the HF band, they were subject to atmospheric skip. This meant that you might be able to talk to the local ranger station ten miles away, or you might get in touch with someone much farther away. On one occasion, we reached an army detachment in Korea operating on the same government frequency that we were using.

The reliability of communications with any of these radios was questionable. Many times we operated either at or outside their designed capability range. At times, when working with the military on aircraft crash sites, we were issued small survival radios weighing a pound or two. Once, when responding to a crash in the Olympic mountains, Dr. Otto Trott was offered his choice of a handset portable at ten pounds, or a survival radio. After a moment of thought, he replied "If I have to carry a radio that doesn't work, let it be the light one."

The first Seattle Mountain Rescue Council truck, a 1941 Army ambulance, had a surplus State Patrol radio that was converted by Irv Herrigstad to operate on an HF distress frequency and put out about sixty watts. It was powered by two dynamotors (a self-contained electric motor and generator system) with very high current consumption. The truck, which had a six-volt electrical system, was also equipped with a motor-driven siren having similar current needs. If the radio was keyed at the same time the siren was blown, the truck would stall because of insufficient voltage to the ignition. With this radio, we could talk to a base station in Seattle, or, on occasion, a Coast Guard station in Adak, Alaska.

As time progressed, I made arrangements with Washington State Patrol Lieutenant Dick Quantz to borrow one or more of their portables for use in the field whenever we had an operation. This was handy, because the rescue truck was housed in the Washington State Patrol garage adjacent to their radio shop. They also arranged for a portable to be left at the Ediz Hook Coast Guard station so that the chopper would have communications with the Mountain Rescue ground team and with State Patrol vehicles.

On one operation, we made contact with the chopper while it was en route to our accident scene high in the Olympic Mountains. The crew asked how many of us were at the scene, which was some ten miles from the road. We replied that there were twelve of us. He then asked the condition of the patient, and if he could stand a short delay before pickup. We replied that he was stable, and the delay could be tolerated. We soon heard the thump of the chopper, and the crew radioed us, saying they were sorry they couldn't airlift the rescue team out, but they had something that would give us a bit of added energy on a hot day. Upon landing, the door slid open and a box with twelve milkshakes was handed out to the rescue team. They had landed the chopper in a small town at the base of the mountains and picked up the shakes from a local ice creamery. The victim was loaded into the chopper for the ride to the hospital. When he recovered, he became a member of Olympic Mountain Rescue.

Mountain rescue call-outs in Seattle were handled via telephone by a group of rescuers' wives we affectionately referred to as our "Call Girls." On small rescues, it was not uncommon to hear the voice of Ome Daiber saying "Grab yer hat" when you answered. Basic information about the incident was given, and a rendezvous location was set for car pooling.

Al Errington, former SMRC chairman, offered the following excerpt. It is part of a tribute to Matie Daiber, one of the original "Call Girls," that he wrote for the March 2009 SMRC newsletter.

> I first met Matie Daiber in the middle of the night forty years ago, in May 1969. The phone rang that night and a soothing, sweet voice asked me if I'd be available for a search for five missing skiers on Mt. Baker. Her gentle, feminine tone was such that I simply couldn't say no (plus, it was my first chance to go on a real rescue). Over the ensuing years, I was treated to more of Matie's wake-up calls, and, time and time again, found it nearly impossible to say no. These "invitations" were also extended by several other ladies amongst our list of "Call Girls."
>
> Eventually, I became the one calling them to initiate a rescue call-out. I very much enjoy thinking back to those 3 A.M. calls to the Daibers. Either Ome or Matie would answer the phone, and the manner of these two rescue pioneers was a contrast in styles. If Ome answered, we would first have a conversation about the current rescue and how it fit into the historical fabric of mountain rescue. He would draw upon his vast experience and describe similar situations from the past. If Matie answered the phone, she would start extracting facts from me—who, where and when. After I'd given her the information, we would put together a response plan. Matie always left me thinking that I'd made up the entire plan, but I know that her gentle sequence of questions commonly led me to our solution. I can still recall the many times she would say "Al, I wonder if we should . . ." This was Matie's way of drawing attention to a critical step that I had skipped or a piece of important information that I had failed to collect.

Later, some used pagers became available. The Seattle Fire Department agreed to send out the activating tones for the pagers on their dispatch frequency when we were called to a search. This got the group of rescuers designed to be the first to arrive at the scene of an emergency, the Fast Alpine Rescue Team (known as the FART team), rolling.

As time passed, it became evident that the rescue teams needed their own radios and a common operating frequency. This was especially true during the 1960 rescue on Mount McKinley. After a bit of pleading, and assurance that the radios would be returned, I was able to secure several portables from the Washington State Patrol to take to Alaska. Their radio license did not cover operation in Alaska, but it was an emergency, and they said to go ahead and take them. I'm not sure what I signed to get the radios. The radios did perform well, even though extra batteries were required to keep them going. One of the radios was almost left at the base camp on the glacier. While taking down a tent, a team member noticed a piece of stiff wire sticking out of the snow. After a bit of digging, he discovered that the wire was the antenna attached to one of the State Patrol radios. It would have been bad news if we had left it there.

Shortly after that, the Federal Communications Commission created the Special Emergency Radio Service. Frequencies were available in the 155 MHz band, so the radios had shorter antennas, and they were less susceptible to atmospheric skip. There was a category for Rescue Squads and Ambulances, but the restriction that you could have only one portable radio per vehicle-mounted mobile radio was unacceptable. I asked Bob Dietsch, a skier and climber friend who was also the Engineer-in-Charge at the local FCC office, for help. Bob reviewed the rules and advised that if we filed as a disaster relief organization we could have an unlimited number of mobiles, portables, and temporary base stations. Lucky for us, at that time the eligibility requirements for disaster relief organizations were not well-defined. We reasoned that if it was a mountain-related disaster, we were trained, equipped, and qualified to be the disaster relief organization. We chose the frequency of 155.160 MHz, because it was adjacent to a law enforcement frequency, and we thought that they would support our request for frequency coordination.

I filed the Mountain Rescue Association's application for the frequency on the first day that the FCC accepted applications for the Special Emergency Radio Service. Apparently the FCC agreed with our reasoning, and shortly we received one of the first licenses in the nation for 155.160 MHz, which has since become the standard frequency used by search-and-rescue organizations throughout the nation. Our call sign, KBC 877, covered all MRA member units. A numbering and record-keeping system was developed to meet FCC requirements.

Ome Daiber uses a radio in 1954.

Photo courtesy of University of Washington Library,
Special Collections Division

A number of MRA member teams raised funds to purchase new radios, all operating on the 155.160 MHz frequency. This created a large pool of radios that could talk together on joint operations involving several different teams. After noticing our success with the 155.160 MHz radio frequency, several law enforcement and emergency management agencies filed for their own licenses, further expanding the Mountain Rescue interoperability.

In Seattle, a group of taxi radios became surplus and were offered to members at a reasonable price. Work parties were organized to put them on the 155.160 MHz frequency. These radios were Motorola 80Ds, and put out thirty watts of power. In addition to taking a large amount of power from a vehicle's electrical system, they occupied about a cubic foot of space in the trunk. These added radios provided better coordination during rescue planning and put enough traffic on the channel that it discouraged ambulance companies and other eligible groups from licensing on the same channel.

The Seattle Mountain Rescue Council received funding for a high-power base station that became known as "Rescue Seattle." This five hundred-watt station stood seven feet tall and was two feet square at its base. The SMRC wanted to operate the station even though it wasn't yet licensed as a fixed base station. At a quick meeting with our FCC friends, we determined that it was probably a temporary base if it had handles and could be moved. A couple of handles were quickly added, and the station became operational at a residence in south Seattle. Later, Jim Goosman arranged for a permanent location at a City of Seattle radio site in north Seattle and a fixed base license and call sign (KGU 976) were obtained. The station was controlled via leased phone lines to remotes in the homes of several members and at the King County Sheriff's office. This station, on a good day, could be heard in Yakima, and once it was heard in Hood River, Oregon. This added range was great for recalling teams that were en route to missions that had been cancelled.

As time went on, and the MRA license was expanded to cover larger and larger areas, the FCC became concerned about our ability to control the radios of all the teams. As a result, they required individual teams with

Mike Norman and Paul Williams use a Washington State Patrol radio. Photo courtesy of Mike Norman

radios to each apply for their own license covering their specific operating area. The MRA license could still be used for joint operations, and for operations outside a team's licensed operating area.

A further complication arose on a search for a military aircraft because the search area spanned the Canadian border. We checked with our friend at the FCC about operating our radios on the other side of the border, and we learned that it was unlikely that our teams would be detected crossing into Canada. Also, getting Canadian approval to use the radios, even on an emergency basis, was going to be time consuming. We were wrong about the likelihood of teams being detected entering Canada. One team encountered the Canadian Border Patrol within minutes of crossing the border. This was pretty much handled by the Border Patrol "looking the other way" and the search team continuing on. After the search, I met with Canadian officials and, at their suggestion, filed for a Canadian reciprocal license to allow the transport and use of radios covered by the KBC 877 license while inside Canada.

After receiving the Canadian license, I decided to prepare for the same scenario in Mexico. After several letters to Mexico City, I received a reply that it was not possible and that I should deal with the local officials. I then asked the San Diego team if they had any problems taking their radios into Baja on operations, and how they handled it. They replied that, at that time, a gallon of wine to the local fire chief resulted in a "license" being issued to allow use of their radios in Mexico. (This may not work today.)

Olympic Mountain Rescue

Keith Spencer of Olympic Mountain Rescue provided information about the group's history.

Olympic Mountain Rescue was formed in 1957, nearly a decade after the SMRC. It included climbers in a tight fraternity who were so concerned about neophytes venturing unescorted into the hills that they took them along on missions for instruction purposes. As a result, there were few accidents. Among the well-known members during the early years were George Martin, Elvin R. "Bob" Johnson, A.E. "Bremerton" Smith and Paul Crews. This colorful group participated in early unofficial rescue activities and can also be credited with starting the Bremerton climbing tradition, which persists to this day, and which has resulted in the periodic updating by Olympic Mountain Rescue of a comprehensive guidebook about the area. The most recent edition, from 2006, is titled *Olympic Mountains: A Climbing Guide*, and is published by The Mountaineers Books.

After the war, many people discovered the Olympic Mountains, and the accident rate rose accordingly. In the late 1940s and early 1950s, there were a number of climbing accidents in the Olympics, including fatalities on both Mount Anderson and Mount Olympus. The primary event that eventually led to the formation of OMR was undoubtedly the death of Bob Thorson on The Brothers. He was the popular student-body president of Bremerton High School. Naturally, when they learned that he had fallen during a descent, Bremerton climbers volunteered to go to the aid of the mortally injured Thorson. These climbers immediately discovered that rescue was a totally different experience than nice, uneventful mountaineering. They had neither adequate training nor proper equipment, which inevitably caused many problems. It was later reported that the group was fortunate to eventually make the recovery without having their own accident.

George Martin, a veteran climber and later the registrar at Olympic College, was disturbed not only by the senselessness of the accident (Thorson and his climbing partners were inexperienced and untrained), but also by the inadequacy of the rescue effort. Thorson had lingered after the fall, and some felt that a timely rescue might have made the difference. At any rate, Martin decided to do something about the problem. He convinced the Olympic College administration that people were going into the mountains with or without training, and that they should offer a mountaineering course to provide the training. This was no small feat, because the idea met with considerable local opposition. Several key Bremerton climbers were opposed to a class that would encourage "reckless" youths to take up mountaineering. The course proved successful from two standpoints. First, very few local climbers have, through the years, been involved in accidents. Second, within a very short time, the course produced a number of skilled climbers who were soon to become the nucleus of Olympic Mountain Rescue.

One evening in January 1957, a small group of local climbers met in George Martin's living room to discuss the practicality of forming a rescue group. Dorrell Looff, chairman of the SMRC, was invited to outline problems that a new rescue group would have to face and to assure Seattle support of the proposed endeavor. The principal output of this meeting was the election of an organizational committee consisting of Roy Etten, Glenn Kelsey, George Martin, Dr. Arpad Masley and Jack Newman. They were charged with the task of developing recommendations regarding type of organization, affiliation, officers, committees, and patch requirements.

After several committee meetings, the complete group reconvened on February 7, 1957, in what proved to be the first official meeting of the new organization. The recommendations made by the committee were quickly reviewed and accepted, and a slate of officers was elected. Grocery man Roy Etten was named the group's first chairman. "Tiger" Jack Newman became vice chairman, and Scout executive George Sainsbury was tapped as secretary-treasurer. Other officers and committee heads were: Arnold Bloomer, Arthur Broetje, Roy Harniss, Jack Hayes, George Martin and Chet Ullin. The group agreed to affiliate with the SMRC, assuming the name Mountain Rescue Council, Olympic Unit, later shortened to Olympic Mountain Rescue. While all these organizational activities were happening, a Navy plane crashed near Kingston, and members of OMR actually participated in its first mission (a search for this aircraft) before the group officially existed.

These early years were the most enjoyable in OMR's history. There were few rules, little red tape, and great camaraderie. Each crisis was met as a call to arms, with the group sallying forth with little more than a primitive stretcher and a first aid kit. However, the period was not all positive. In addition to the group's lack of equipment and training, group members came from diverse backgrounds. They were a strong-spoken, hard-nosed bunch, with definite opinions. There was more than one tough battle about how things should be done. Chairman Etten had his hands full, and years later confided that his two years as chairman were among the most difficult in his life. He also noted that, on several occasions, he half expected the combatants to attack each other. But no blows were ever struck.

The early meetings were a little strange by current standards; quite informal and basically fun to attend. Many unusual things happened. Kent Heathershaw stood up during one meeting to request OMR help in providing leadership to the Olympic College rescue and survival class. Kent had been attending the meetings, but had not been particularly speedy about formally joining the group. The group arose en masse to silence the speech, saying that only paid-up members could speak of serious matters. While a bewildered Kent Heathershaw looked on, George Martin and Chuck Maiden each offered a dollar to pay his dues. Heathershaw was then allowed to proceed, and the group enthusiastically supported his idea.

Olympic Mountain Rescue is still operating today, with twenty-five active members and an excellent working relationship with local sheriffs and the rangers at Olympic National Park. Although based in Kitsap County, it regularly responds to missions in Mason, Jefferson, and Clallam counties, and other areas within the State of Washington.

Tacoma Mountain Rescue

John Simac, Ken Capron and Gus Bush provided information about Tacoma Mountain Rescue's beginnings.

Initially named the Tacoma Unit of the Mountain Rescue Council, Tacoma Mountain Rescue was formed by a group of local climbers who had already been carrying out rescue missions as individuals. They all recognized that other established rescue units were often busy or otherwise unavailable to assist with local incidents. The problem was discussed, and the unit was formed in November of 1958. Many of these climbers were members of the Tacoma chapter of The Mountaineers who were ready and willing to help. One climber, Owen Wright, spearheaded the drive to organize these interested individuals, which included the following listed charter members in addition to Wright: Cliff Cooley, Bruce Galloway, James Holt, Charles Kilmer, Robert

Koster, George Munday, Barry Palmer, Glen Robertson, Lester Robinson, John Simac, Lee Tegner, Scott Wesley, Mary Francis Wright, and Mary Joan Wright.

Most requests for a rescue response came from the local authorities, but some came from word-of-mouth through The Mountaineers, and were then passed on to those who were willing to help. Early call-outs relied on the use of phone trees to notify unit members and initiate the needed response to the situation. The Tacoma unit had a very strong base and, in the early years, had as many as forty members, many of whom remained active for years. The average age of the rescuers was about thirty-five, but younger climbers were also allowed to join the group, as long as they had a respected member to recommend their admittance. All members had to have Board approval to enter the unit, and they had to pay dues, own their own equipment, use their own vehicles, and financially support their involvement with the group. Members were required to be physically, technically, and mentally prepared for any type of mission. These missions could and did involve almost anything, including, but not limited to, high-angle and high-altitude rescue, evidence searches, and missing persons searches. Those on the active roster were expected to attend trainings, which were conducted monthly, and to assist in as many rescues as possible.

Monthly trainings were usually set up as mock missions, and, if possible, were also used as a debrief session for a prior mission. Members would discuss and practice what went right and talk about what they could have done better. It appears that the unit was most often able to field as many rescuers as the situation required, and ten to twelve members seemed to be the norm. The Tacoma unit was also the first in the region to have female climbers as part of a field rescue team. The team relied heavily on an "in-town coordinator" while out on missions, much as they still do today, to provide additional resources and manpower. The coordinator would also keep the families of the rescuers updated about the events of the mission, and the potential return time of the unit members. Rescuers' family members seemed to be very involved in the group. They provided important support to the team and its members.

Tacoma Mountain Rescue members used The Mountaineers' clubhouse as their meeting facility until 1975, when they were able to secure their own building. Safety and education were always a major

Governor Albert Rosellini and Ome Daiber.
Photo by the author

part of the unit's mission, and many members conducted classes, ran seminars, provided medical trainings, and helped educate the public whenever the opportunity arose. Many members of the unit were Emergency Medical Technicians. The ability to obtain EMT status by attending certain trainings offered by the group was also a draw that attracted new members. Some rescuers, including John Simac and Lee Tegner, were made deputy sheriffs or deputy coroners, complete with badges, in order to streamline missions that included a deceased subject. Team members would often be transported by military aircraft to an accident scene, and were assisted by a military pararescue group when required. That group would also help with communications and request assistance from other rescue units as the need arose. This led to Tacoma Mountain Rescue being a charter member of the national Mountain Rescue Association.

On average, the unit would be involved in ten to fourteen major rescue situations in any given year. One such mission included traveling to Alaska and assisting in a big rescue on Mount McKinley in May of 1960. Other major accomplishments included helping start the Washington State Emergency Management program in 1964 as well as an EMT program in 1973. Another big event was a training that involved solving a rigging problem as Washington Governor Albert Rosellini looked on. This training was designed and conducted in order to demonstrate to the governor the value and potential of a mountain rescue team. Many team members were also instrumental in the creation and construction of the Camp Schurman climber's hut on Mount Rainier in 1959.

The men and women who were involved in the unit's conception and during its early years were very committed, and they created a strong and sound organization. The unit continues to play a critical role in assisting state authorities in conducting the search-and-rescue operations they perform. The fact that the Tacoma Mountain Rescue Unit is still in operation fifty years after its founding is definite proof of the hard work and effort of those original members.

A Tacoma Mountain Rescue Training

An account of an early Tacoma Mountain Rescue training written by John Simac was included in the April 7, 1960 edition of the SMRC newsletter:

> The Tacoma unit had an idea. They picked a big cliff; invited some big people; and got some big help from the Seattle and Olympic Mountain rescue units. The result was a simulated rescue extravaganza. Even the weather was in our favor. The plan was to use pararescue, hot food drop, ground support for litter evacuation, and to lower two litters over a 200 foot vertical cliff; one lowered by a Tacoma team, the other by an Olympic team. The Seattle team set up an aerial tram. While all this was going on, Tacoma's public relations man, along with an SMRC ambassador, were busy answering questions about rescue techniques. Official guests included: Governor Albert D. Rosellini; Director of Aeronautics William Gebinini; the Commanding General of the Washington State National Guard, Major General George M. Haskett; Pierce County Director of Civil Defense Gus K. Partridge; the Pierce County Sheriff, Frank Stojack; Chief of Washington State Patrol, Roy Betlach; Rescue Officer of McChord Field, Captain Costello; representatives of the Forest Service and Weyerhaeuser Timber Co.; the Press and, of course, our own photographer.
>
> The purpose of the practice was to demonstrate to State and local officials the potential and the capabilities of the mountain rescue units. The whole operation was successful. The pararescue was accurate, and our pilot did a fine job of flying and dropping cargo. Comments from officials and laymen were very gratifying. Follow-up action is being taken to arrange a meeting of the various agencies participating in an actual rescue, to promote greater cooperation among all rescue agencies, to understand their problems and limitations, and to discover where the overlap in authority is.
>
> Thanks, fellows, for a job well done!

Everett Mountain Rescue

Formed in 1956 by a group of mountaineers, the Everett Mountain Rescue Unit (later shortened to Everett Mountain Rescue) was one of the

founding organizations of the MRA. Information about its history was
provided by Scott Welton, the 2008 Chairman of EMR.

Mountain climbing in the Pacific Northwest started to become
popular after World War II, with the return of the 10th Mountain
Division from Europe and Fred Beckey's evangelism of the sport. With
more people venturing into the wilderness, more people started
thinking, "What do we do if something happens?" This increased
awareness was one of the factors contributing to the creation of
mountain rescue organizations and other groups providing formalized
wilderness training. European organizations were already in existence,
and experiences with those groups influenced the beginnings of the
organizations affiliated with the SMRC.

EMR, under the leadership of Kenn Carpenter, was founded in 1954
as a result of an ad hoc mission to search for a group of The
Mountaineers that had been stranded by the weather on Mount
Stickney. Friends and family members coordinated the rescue efforts.
EMR was an individual entity closely associated with the SMRC, and
was often referred to by that organization as the Everett unit. Eventually,
EMR, together with the SMRC and other sister organizations, joined
together to formally organize the MRA.

Carpenter had been friends with Ome Daiber, who had founded the
SMRC and was a key focal point for mountain rescue in the Pacific
Northwest. Kenn had numerous conversations with Ome about starting
a rescue group that would serve the northern portions of Washington
state. Everett Mountain Rescue started with nineteen eager volunteers
with no equipment in 1954, and grew to include more than one hundred
members and a new rescue truck by 1964. During this time, Carpenter
was the secretary of the SMRC as well as the Chairman of EMR. He
worked at coordinating the different regional mountain rescue units into
what would eventually become the MRA.

On October 15, 1956, EMR sponsored its first coordinated training
for seventy rescue men and women from throughout the region at
Mount Erie, Washington. Carpenter, Dean Perkins, and others were
credited with the success of the day in the field. Rescue activities were
explained and demonstrated by Pete Schoening (cables for raising or
lowering victims, a man carrying an injured person on his back in a
sling); Ralph Johnson (knot-tying and a carabiner brake); Bill Unsoeld
(the meaning of mechanical advantage and the use of pulleys); Jim

Whittaker (lowering a stretcher down a cliff); and Ward Irwin (crevasse rescue and glacier travel).

During this same period, Carpenter was approached by Bill Cross from the state Department of Civil Defense about EMR joining that organization in order to fall under its insurance umbrella. EMR started meeting in the Civil Defense facilities that were in the basement of the old county seat, across the street from Everett City Hall. Civil Defense also stored sixty-thousand square feet of military surplus gear for use in case of a national emergency. Everett Mountain Rescue also built a relationship with the Everett Rotary Club through Ralph Mackey, whose family founded and promoted Washington Stove Works. This relationship assisted in fundraising and the acquisition of the first EMR truck and the unit's first specialized litter from Austria.

In cooperation with the SMRC, EMR, The Mountaineers of Seattle, and the Everett branch of The Mountaineers, classes in mountaineering were offered at Everett Community College.

Today, Everett Mountain Rescue is an independent non-profit organization that works seamlessly with Snohomish County Volunteer Search and Rescue, as well as other mountain rescue units and search-and-rescue units in Washington State. More than three hundred members have passed through the doors since the group's inception. EMR continues to build upon the same high standards that have followed the team from the beginning. Through countless hours of volunteerism, caring, and training, many lives have been saved.

Mount St. Helens Ski Patrol and Rescue Unit

This small rescue unit was activated in 1948 in the Kelso-Longview area of Washington by Rob and Val Quoidback. The group's principal search-and-rescue and ski-patrol operations were devoted to year-round search and rescue in the area of Mount St. Helens. Rob and his brother Val became members of the National Ski Patrol (numbers 1000 and 1002), and in the 1950s they became affiliated with the Seattle Mountain Rescue Council by participating in some rescues and body recoveries. In 1960, the Quoidbacks served in the Squaw Valley Olympics Ski Patrol. Rob climbed Mount St. Helens ninety-six times before the 1980 eruption, and sixteen times since. The brothers operated the Quoidback Construction Company in Longview. Val passed away in 2001, and Rob was eighty-four when he contacted me about this book and provided this information.

I first met the Quoidbacks during a winter weekend at the unit's small cabin in the woods near timberline, and I recall us all having to dig down through the snow and enter through an improvised tunnel that served as both chimney and entry door. I last saw Val during a rescue operation on Mount St. Helens in the 1960s.

Central Washington Mountain Rescue

An article written by Lex Maxwell and updated by Lynn Buchanan provided the following information about the forming of Central Washington Mountain Rescue.

Central Washington Mountain Rescue was established in the mid-1950s in response to the urgings of Ome Daiber and Wolf Bauer, who had often traveled to the eastern Cascades to participate in rescue efforts. Lex Maxwell of Yakima, although quite involved in numerous other civic activities, managed to pull together a group of climbing and skiing friends to start a rescue unit in the Yakima area. Lewis Newhall, an ardent National Ski Patrol member, agreed to accept the initial chairmanship of the group. He was a very dedicated leader, and would drive all night to attend rescue meetings in Seattle to bring back information and share experiences with CWMR members.

The new unit's early needs were many. Personnel needed to be trained in evacuation techniques, mountaineering first aid, teamwork, and how to cooperate with civil authorities and other rescue units. They needed money to buy litters, ropes, first-aid supplies and radios. They were eventually able to raise the money. Fundraising and training were long, hard, and sometimes thankless tasks, but whenever the group received a call for help and everything was available and ready to go, it stimulated their efforts with a new urgency. Media publicity was helpful, because it mentioned the names of those involved in the organization and those supporting it.

Marcel Schuster was an important asset to CWMR. Before World War II, Schuster had been in the Bergwacht, a group of mountain guides in Germany who served as a mountain rescue unit. After serving during the war in the German mountain troops, Schuster came to America and was able to share invaluable European rescue techniques with the unit. In addition to Lewis Newhall and Maxwell, early chairmen of the rescue unit included Bob McCall, Hal Foss and Lynn Buchanan. One of the first things they did was develop a procedure manual, which each member kept near the telephone, and which the group also supplied to the Sheriff and Forest Service offices. Another big step was to get similar rescue units established in Ellensburg, under the leadership of Gene Prater and others; and in Wenatchee, under the leadership of Dr. Don Fager.

During the early years, CWMR developed some complex arrangements with the state Department of Civil Defense, ham radio operators, and other organizations that could assist them. The ham radio groups were trained in communications, had the equipment needed for operations, and formed an excellent statewide resource during many rescues. Civil Defense had staff and equipment available, and offered disability insurance to members in case of an accident.

However, there was always the haunting fear of a lawsuit being filed against unit members as the result of a mistake or perceived negligence. So, at one of CWMR's meetings with the Seattle Mountain Rescue Council, Maxwell discussed the issue with Paul Williams, a Seattle attorney and SMRC member. Paul recommended that CWMR affiliate with the Seattle Mountain Rescue Council. This would allow the CWMR team to enjoy the same corporate shelter the Seattle group had. Paul worked out the needed resolution, and CWMR became the Central Washington Unit of the Mountain Rescue Council. Thereafter, a CMWR member would always be a member of the SMRC Board of Directors, until CWMR became an independent unit. After a few years of serving in that board position, Maxwell grew tired of driving back and forth to Seattle, so Lynn Buchanan agreed to serve.

The Washington Region of the MRA

When the national Mountain Rescue Association first formed, its regions were rather informal, but eventually there was growing pressure for the teams in the MRA to organize into formal regions. The Washington region included a team or two from Canada, but there was very little contact with them. In 1968, the various member teams in Washington put together a committee headed by Charles Crenshaw and Lynn Buchanan to draw up by-laws and formally organize the region,

including only teams within the state. Most of the teams from
Washington started as sub-units of Seattle Mountain Rescue Council,
but as the teams got better organized, they each became incorporated,
developed their own by-laws and worked with their local Sheriff's office,
inviting other teams to help as they were needed for larger missions. The
Washington teams formally adopted the recommendations of the
committee in 1970 and became the Washington Mountain Rescue
Association, which had its own board of officers and held meetings a
couple of times each year to prepare for the national MRA business
meetings. Charles Crenshaw was the first president of the region,
followed by Lynn Buchanan. Lynn later went on to become Chairman
of the MRA and Mayor of Yakima.

CHAPTER 9

History of Mountain Rescue Units in Oregon

Andy Anderson's wife jokingly inferred they were "just a bunch of rats climbing around on the crags on weekends, instead of staying home with their families." The men realized that with all the publicity [surrounding a high-profile search], the news media would be waiting for them on their return, so they were prepared when the reporters asked if they belonged to any particular group. "Yes—the Crag Rats," they replied.

EINO ANNALA
(1976)

Crag Rats of Hood River

Information about the formation of the Crag Rats of Hood River, Oregon, was procured primarily from an article written by Esther K. Smith published August 23, 2006 in the *Hood River News.*

On August 3, 1926, in Hood River, Oregon, a meeting of the Mountain Goats, an informal group of local mountaineers, was held to discuss the need for a local mountain rescue group. The initial meeting of this small group of outdoors enthusiasts was arranged by lumberman A. L. Anderson. This meeting marked the beginning of the Hood River-based Crag Rats. In 2006, club members celebrated the 80th birthday of their group, which is the oldest such organization in the United States.

According to an article in the August 27, 1926 edition of the *Hood River News*, the organization got its semi-official start on August 23, 1926, when a committee made up of Anderson, Kent Shoemaker, and L. M. Baldwin drew up bylaws and a constitution, and proposed the nomination of officers.

According to charter member Eino Annala in his 1976 book, *The Crag Rats*, the group's name can be credited to one of the member's wives. The meeting Andy had called for August 3 did not produce a name, although several had been considered. One that received a good deal of consideration was Crag Rats. It seems that Delia, Andy Anderson's wife, jokingly suggested it, inferring they were "just a bunch of rats climbing around on the crags on the weekends, instead of staying home with their families." That meeting was adjourned until the end of the month, but on August 16, an event occurred that definitely settled the matter. Mace Baldwin, Percy Bucklin, and Jess Puddy found seven-year-old Jackie Strong on the west slopes of Mount Hood. The search was on its third day and had drawn a great deal of publicity and more than 250 searchers. Soldiers from the 7th Infantry Division, Mazamas, Trails Club members, Hood River Guides, Forest Service rangers, police, sheriff's deputies, mountaineers, and the Gresham neighbors of the Strongs were either searching or hurrying to join the search when rifle shots from higher on the mountain indicated the boy had been found.

The rescuers realized that the search was very high-profile, so reporters would likely be waiting to talk to them when they got back. They were prepared, and when the media representatives asked if they belonged to any particular group, they had an answer.

"Yes—the Crag Rats," they replied. The name was officially adopted at an organizational meeting on August 30, 1926, where officers were also elected. Mace Baldwin held the first post of "Big Squeak," and Andy Anderson became the "Little Squeak."

A September 10, 1926 *Hood River News* article included the group's membership criteria: "No one can be a member who has not climbed Mount Hood and Mount Adams and must climb at least one mountain each year to keep in good standing." Crag Rats membership is by invitation only and requires a unanimous vote by the membership.

The Strong rescue and another well-publicized rescue that happened soon after brought the Crag Rats much attention, but it was never attention they sought. In fact, Baldwin, Bucklin and Puddy turned down medals that a jeweler in Portland had offered as a reward to whoever found the lost Strong boy, saying that they did not care to receive medals for what they had done.

Annala wrote in his book about the group that, during the 1920s and 1930s, the Crag Rats were eulogized in newspapers and magazines all over the country, and that he remembered when a letter from an author who was writing a text book for school children was read at one of their regular meetings. The author wanted stories about "modern heroes." The members discussed the letter very briefly, and instructed the group's secretary to thank the author, but that they were not heroes.

Over the years, the Crag Rats have been involved in countless rescues and recoveries, and have also managed to work in some play time on the mountain. For many years, they held the record for "first climb of the year" of Mount Hood. In the early days, their play dates on the mountain included baseball games on skis.

The Crag Rats built their original Crag Rat Hut, which stood on the rocks above Interstate 84's Exit 62 (the stone fireplace, all that remains, is still visible), in 1932, and used it until 1966, when the present hut was built, high on the hill east of Pine Grove School. Since 1954, the Crag Rats have also been stewards of the historical Cloud Cap Inn, on the north side of Mount Hood, by special permit from the Forest Service. The group has restored and improved the site in the fifty-plus years since it took over its care.

From its twenty-four original members, the group has grown to about one hundred, sixty of which are active in search and rescue. Some members are third-generation Crag Rats, such as those from the Hukari, Sheppard, and Wells families.

As Annala said at the end of his 1976 book, "The Crag Rats are not in the public eye as much as they were for so many years. They are members of larger mountain rescue groups, which naturally receive the publicity connected with rescues in our mountains. But you can rest assured that usually in the rescue operations will be seen men with black-and-white checkered shirts; the men Delia Anderson dubbed the Crag Rats."

The Wy'east Climbers

The history of the Wy'east Climbers is described in Ric Conrad's 2003 unpublished manuscript, *Mount Hood: Adventures of the Wy'east Climbers.*

The Wy'east Climbers club was formed in December of 1930 to unite a select group of the most adventurous and skilled mountaineers in Oregon. Many were members of the Crag Rats and Mazamas, but rather than hike in parties that numbered more than a dozen people, they preferred to climb in small parties and seek new, challenging routes on Mount Hood and other peaks in the Northwest.

Over the years, the Wy'east Climbers have been described as haughty, dangerous, stunt climbers, and self-serving eccentrics. They were labeled as dangerous merely because they pushed the limits of mountaineering on Mount Hood further than any previous generation. They attempted and succeeded on routes that their predecessors had deemed unclimbable. With relatively few exceptions, all of their first ascents were the work of careful planning and physical preparation. To call the Wy'easters self-serving runs counter to the fact that for decades they either led or were members of nearly all the search-and-rescue missions in and around their area. They were the creators of the Mount Hood Ski Patrol, and all members were required to take first aid courses so that they could assist any injured climber.

Perhaps the only negative description that has any bearing would be elitist. But members are willing to concede the perfectly understandable pride they feel in regards to their organization. The group had the toughest admission requirements in the country at the time, and it was only natural that members felt a healthy sense of self-esteem after being asked to join such a tight-knit and skilled fraternity. They are elitist, perhaps, but not entirely exclusive. Among Wy'easters who also were members of the Mazamas were such notables as Ray Atkeson, Everett Darr, Joe Leuthold, Hank Lewis, Ole Lien, Randall Kester, and Keith Petrie. And members didn't restrict their climbing partnerships to other Wy'easters. Bill Hackett was never a Wy'east Climber, but Russ McJury formed a fast friendship with him and they became one of the most accomplished teams in the Oregon Cascades. Hackett and McJury were veterans of the Army's 10th Mountain Division.

The Wy'easters had a right to be proud of their accomplishments. In 1930, there were only three standard routes to the summit of Mount Hood. The skilled and determined Wy'easters re-opened or helped pioneer six new routes on the mountain in as many years, with the routes ranging from mere rock scrambles to challenging vertical headwalls. Jim Mount and Everett Darr re-opened the Wy'east Route in 1932, a path not taken since the Langille Brothers took it in the 1890s. Ralph Calkin and Jim Mount made the first ascent, in 1932, of what today is called the Leuthold Couloir. Russ McJury and Bill Hackett opened up a new route on the northeast face in 1936. McJury and Joe Leuthold pioneered the virgin Sandy Glacier Headwall in 1937 and the Eliot Glacier Headwall the following year. McJury and Gary Leech also made the 1936 round-the-mountain ski trip, the first high-altitude encirclement of Mount Hood.

Members of the Wy'east Climbers also put up new routes throughout the Cascade Range and Columbia River Gorge. Their most significant first ascents were the Jefferson Park Glacier Route on Mount Jefferson in 1933, by Everett Darr and Jim Mount; the Battlement Ridge on Mount Adams by the same pair in 1933; the Klickitat Glacier Route on Mount Adams in 1938, by Joe Leuthold, Russ McJury, and Wendall Stout; the South Side Route on Mount Washington in 1940, by Ralph Calkin, Everett Darr and Jim Mount; St. Peter's Dome in the Columbia Gorge in 1940, by Joe Leuthold, Everett Darr, Jim Mount and others; the Northwest Face of Three Fingered Jack in 1941, by Joe Leuthold and Everett Darr; and the Northwest Ridge of the same peak in 1942, by Eldon Metzger and Everett and Ida Darr. Perhaps the most significant ascent, with the exception of St. Peter's Dome, was the South Face of Mount Washington in 1940, by Ralph Calkin, Jim Mount, Eldon Metzger and the Darrs.

Bill Hackett noted that he had never known a group of more humble individuals in his life. He could never understand why they didn't publish their achievements and gain recognition for their first ascents. To this day, few in the Pacific Northwest mountaineering community are aware of just how much the club accomplished in such a short period of time. Very few members of the Mazamas are even aware that their library holds the originally published bulletins of the Wy'east Climbers. If not for the efforts of historians like Fred McNeil, Jack Grauer, and Ray Conkling, much of the history of the Wy'easters would have been lost.

The Wy'east Climbers should also be remembered for their willingness to help their fellow climbers above timberline. Barrie James, one of the group's charter members, built two portable radio sets for use in emergency situations on the mountain. They each weighed a phenomenal twenty-six pounds, but they had a range of thirty miles and came in handy on a number of occasions. After A. J. Johanns donated a dilapidated toboggan to the Wy'easters, Curtis Ijames set about rebuilding it for rescue work. Early members of the club ensured that a proper knowledge of first aid was a requirement for membership. They attended mandatory courses in Portland as well as in Government Camp, becoming the most proficient rescue workers in the area. In reference to those early years, Everett Darr said:

> Originally organized in the interest of public safety and rescue work on Mount Hood and adjacent peaks, fellowship has flourished among the membership, and a unified, coordinated power of accomplishment is the result. We have been called to the mountains on many emergencies, and every man has responded. We know the dangers and discomforts of mountaineering as well as the pleasures. We have seen one of our own men cast to his death by a great peak. But such disasters have not swerved the club from its purpose or loosened its morale. They only tend to tighten the bonds that hold it together. We are proud of our record. The good work will be continued.

In many ways, this group represented the type of club we all wish we could belong to. Difficult enough entrance requirements to give you a sense of satisfaction if you were allowed in, yet requirements that could be met with enough skill, patience and determination. They looked out after one another, both physically and spiritually. They were friends, pals, and wartime comrades who shared a similar history and background. When Joe Leuthold's leadership skills came under fire, for instance, following the Mazamas first winter attempt on Mount Hood in 1938, Curtis Ijames stepped up and publicly denounced his detractors. Ijames drafted a lengthy paper on the subject, one that clearly exonerated Leuthold while admonishing his critics for jumping to conclusions before they had performed any research.

The Wy'east Climbers thrived on pushing the limits of mountaineering. They didn't believe any mountain or route was impossible, and avidly set out to conquer new terrain. They studied the weather, the ice, and the crumbling rock towers that made up Mount Hood. They sought every advantage available to reach the summit. They experimented with equipment, clothing and provisions. Several of them moved to the base of the mountain in order to have more time for exploration. They ushered in a twenty-year period of exploration and achievement. Individuals from the Wy'east Climbers participated in a number of searches and rescues in the region, typical of the volunteer clubs like the Crag Rats, who informally showed up on the early missions.

The Wy'easters themselves look back and smile whenever they discuss the Golden Age. "People need to understand," Hank Lewis said during a 2008 interview, "that during the Depression, we worked six days a week and couldn't get away for a whole weekend like you can today. We also didn't have these superhighways you see everywhere. It took a lot longer to get from one place to the next and with only a day off a week, we were forced to remain in the Cascades and focus our energies on the nearby crags. We had to pack a whole weekend of living into a single day, and boy, we sure did!"

Lu Norene, who spent a great deal of time on the mountain during the Second World War, recalls that escapism was pretty important in those days. "We were always reading some pretty depressing headlines," he says. "It was so nice just to forget our troubles for a day and head into the hills. What a great bunch of guys. Honest, hardworking, and fellows who would always volunteer their time and talent whenever a climber was in trouble. Days on the mountain, nights in the Blue Ox Bar! They were great days to be on the mountain."

The Alpinees of Hood River

The Alpinees, Inc. was organized on February 3, 1947, for the purpose of operating and maintaining a mountain rescue organization that would work to promote, develop, and advance general and scientific information and knowledge in mountain climbing and mountain rescue work. They were also interested in advancing and teaching winter sports. Charter members were L. C. "Jack" Baldwin, George Howell, Myron Weygandt, Dick Mansfield, Don Kresse, and Bob Duckwall. It was this writer's pleasure in the 1950s to visit with Baldwin at his home in Hood River.

The organizers were young, vigorous men, who had just returned from duty in World War II. Two were also new members of the Crag Rats who wanted more action and greater use of current techniques in mountaineering. The club quickly became aligned with the SMRC.

The group soon acquired a bergtrage (German-style litter) for evacuation of accident victims, and developed a very effective cable retrieval system, which is still in use today. On May 19, 1957, The Alpinees presented an impressive demonstration and simulated rescue on Armed Forces Day at the Portland Air Base. Many other such presentations were made at mountain rescue conferences, such as one at Snoqualmie Pass, Washington, on May 25, 1949. An exhibition was made to the ranger staff at Yosemite National Park in early October of 1958, when Jack Baldwin, Roger Getchell, Ernest Hanson, Cranson Fosberg, Harold Franz, and Paul Tyler visited the park.

The Alpinees Club was affiliated with the Senior Member Group of the Hood River Squadron of the Civil Air Patrol's Oregon Wing. This is a unique arrangement that resulted in remarkable strengthening of both components. The Alpinees' activities pumped new life into the waning squadron, and air support gave the club a very effective tool for search-and-rescue work. Many of their operations have involved searching for downed aircraft and rescuing survivors. Searching rivers for drowning victims has been an important function, also. In mountain rescue work, The Alpinees have been extremely active: keyed into radio networks, and ready to go at a moment's notice. The club includes aircraft pilots, experienced climbers, boaters, radio operators, 4-wheel-drive vehicle operators, skiers, and first aid practitioners. In 1954, the National Ski Patrol formally gave The Alpinees the authority to act as Mount Hood Ski Patrol on the north side of the mountain.

The club acquired a square acre of land on the southern outskirts of Hood River, and in 1961, they began clearing this timbered plot and planning a building. Jack Baldwin, who was a building contractor, supervised the erection of The Alpinees' home, completed late in 1962. The structure is uniquely suited to the club's use. A forty-foot fireplace made of stone can be climbed by several routes. Anchors at the top of the fireplace allow a belayer to protect climbers as they negotiate the wall. Group members can even practice walking a loaded akia down the vertical surface in a simulated rescue.

Like the Crag Rats, The Alpinees are a closely welded group of individuals. Once each month, an indoor lecture and training session is given at the club house. The subjects include advanced work as well as frequent reinforcement of basic mountaineering, first aid, and search techniques. Frequent outdoor practice sessions are scheduled. The group's training officer at this writing is Carroll Davis.

The Alpinees membership numbers about one hundred today. New members need not have a background of experience, but are expected to learn search-and-rescue techniques as soon as possible. Many of the new members are young, which presages a continuing vitality in the club. Some of the better mountaineers in the group are Carroll Davis, Kenneth Abendroth, Darryl Lloyd, Dean Kleinsmith, Tom Nash, Bob Newman, Howard Kanable, Jack Baldwin, and James Parr.

The Mountain Rescue and Safety Council of Oregon

Information about The Mountain Rescue and Safety Council of Oregon was gathered primarily from Christopher Van Tilburg's *Mountain Rescue Doctor* (2007).

The need for mountain rescue in Oregon increased as the years passed, and it became apparent that a greater statewide coordination between the Crag Rats, The Alpinees, The Wy'east Climbers and members of the Mazamas was necessary to increase the effectiveness of rescue efforts. Initially, leaders in these units, along with members of the Mount Hood Ski Patrol, joined to form the Central Rescue Committee and Emergency Rescue Group. But still there were problems due to the lack of a formal organization. By early 1955, there was considerable interest in coordinating the work of a great number of outdoors activists, local and college clubs, local governmental agencies, and even the Boy Scouts and Civil Air Patrol, under one umbrella.

Representatives of these clubs met in the summer of 1955 and discussed the need for greater public education about the hazards of year-round mountain travel, and training in mountain survival techniques. Finally, on October 12, 1955, after a couple days of glacier training on the Eliot Glacier, the Mountain Rescue and Safety Council of Oregon was formed during an evening meeting at Cloud Cap Inn. MRSCO's articles of incorporation had been created a few weeks earlier by James Simmons, Dick Pooley, and John Biewener. Directors were chosen from several participating clubs: Pooley from the Mazamas, Randall Kester of the Wy'east Climbers, and Ross Hukari of the Crag Rats.

On November 10, 1955, MRSCO held its first board meeting in Portland, and elected Randall Kester as president, Hukari as vice-president, Biewener as secretary-treasurer, Pooley as education chairman, and Hank Lewis as rescue chairman. The rescue chairman was actually the most important member of the organization, and Lewis' background included being the first salaried patrol chief of the Mount Hood Ski Patrol. Hank was a veteran of many searches and rescues, and today, at the age of ninety-seven, he's still very active and sharp. He was at the reunion of MRA founding members at Timberline Lodge in July 2008.

As in Seattle, the early call-outs for searches or rescues in the Portland area were done very informally. Dick Pooley recalls that Jim Simmons in Portland had a list in his desk of qualified people, and, when he would get word of a person injured or missing in the mountains, he would start making calls. In most cases, these were people who were affiliated with MRSCO or one of the volunteer clubs mentioned earlier in this chapter. Pooley also remembers when Explorer Scouts were organized to perform some basic work in the mountains, and that they were very effective. To this day, Explorer Search and Rescue is an important part of the emergency response network in the Pacific Northwest, which is one of the few places in the country where these units exist.

MRSCO held numerous meetings and training sessions over the years. In 1957, it was decided that every rescue member must have a basic Red Cross First Aid card by 1958, and an Advanced First Aid card by 1959. Training sessions were held at Santiam Pass in 1958, at Paradise Valley on Mount Rainier in 1961, and at Smith Rocks in 1965. Almost all rescues and searches were followed by meetings of the teams and the survivors, if possible. Operations were thoroughly critiqued and errors and omissions were noted in order to constantly upgrade the quality of their operations.

By 1975, MRSCO still functioned as an operating unit, but business was down. Multnomah and Clackamas Counties had rescue personnel on staff in their law-enforcement departments. If a rescue was called for, local sheriffs usually responded. Searches were conducted mostly by well-trained Explorer Scouts. Other rescue units were formed in Eugene and Corvallis, and they became more closely tied to the national MRA. Eventually, there was much dissent among MRSCO units outside of Portland. By mutual agreement, MRSCO was dissolved, but all local teams maintained their membership in the national Mountain Rescue Association (MRA), which had been established in 1959.

CHAPTER 10

Mountain Rescue Comes of Age

The Establishment of the Mountain Rescue Association at Mount Hood in 1959, and the MRA Today

> *Rescuers risk their lives and limbs to save the*
> *unfortunate victims. [This] does emphasize the*
> *hazardous nature of rescue operations and the need*
> *for a well-trained, well-equipped group.*

THE AMERICAN ALPINE CLUB (1961)

The Establishment of the Mountain Rescue Association

Interviews in 2008 with Dick Pooley, the first president of the Mountain Rescue Association, and minutes from the group's first meetings, provided information about the formation of the MRA.

By 1957, it was becoming clear that some greater coordination would be required between the local volunteer teams that were operating independently in Washington and Oregon. MRSCO and the SMRC were similar in that they were developed with the idea of coordinating local activities within their region. But there were times when Oregon teams were informally called to missions in Washington, and Seattle teams would occasionally be asked to help in Oregon. It also became clear that some missions had requirements for people or equipment that were not available at the local team level. At this stage, there was no governmental regulation or control of mountain rescue activities in Washington or Oregon, save the operations conducted by federal personnel inside the national parks.

In November of 1958, the first "Regional Ad-Hoc Committee" for mountain rescue was formed and a meeting was held in Olympia,

Washington. This was a good location because it was between Seattle and Portland, the centers of much of the rescue activity. Dick Pooley and John Arens were the leading representatives from Portland, and Dorrell Looff, Ome Daiber, and Otto Trott represented Seattle Mountain Rescue Council. The discussion centered on the possibility of imposing minimum requirements for the training of rescuers, such as first aid and helicopter training, which were then new to the rescue scene.

One major point of discussion at these early meetings was the use of a standard mountain rescue logo. The insignia that was adopted had earlier been developed in Seattle by Wolf Bauer. He came up with a very simple logo that included the lifesaving cross done in blue and white, which reminded him of his native Bavaria in the Alps. It was agreed that there was a need to be able to recognize qualified rescuers as soon as they arrived at the scene, and that rescuers had to meet some minimum qualifications to possess this identification. So the Oregon delegates proposed, and the Seattle delegates agreed, that a common patch based on Wolf Bauer's design would be used.

There was much discussion in the early meetings about who would be able to wear the new patch. It was agreed that the term "rescue member" should refer to a person with full qualifications. According to the minutes of the November 16, 1958 meeting, those qualifications included "an advanced first aid card, attendance at board meetings, conferences and/or rescues, and should be able to handle themselves in almost any situation."

The basic groundwork for a new and more formalized association was completed in Olympia on November 16, 1958 at a meeting of the Ad

Three early mountain rescue patches designed by Wolf Bauer.

Hoc Committee. Paul Williams took the lead in drafting a constitution and Dorrell Looff of the SMRC pushed to bring it to the membership for signature.

At a previously scheduled training and meeting at Mount Hood's Timberline Lodge on June 6 and 7, 1959, delegates from the nine volunteer teams, as well as two government units, met and reviewed the proposed Constitution of the MRA. The primary driver behind the drafting was Paul Williams, an SMRC member and attorney. There was no major controversy about the signing of the document. It was recognized by all that the new organization would allow the authority and control of mountain rescues to remain with the local units. The new organization would be more for coordination and education, and setting minimum qualifications and a common insignia for mountain rescuers.

George Sainsbury of SMRC said during a 2008 interview that he recalls that when the constitution was discussed at Timberline Lodge there was a feeling that something important was going on, a "first" for mountain rescue in the United States. George was in the basement of the lodge with a typewriter, writing up the constitution, and Paul Williams would bring the drafts to the group, then back to George for corrections. George's wife was the proofreader. Eventually, an acceptable draft was reached for the delegates to sign.

The first MRA constitution was adopted at Mount Hood on June 7, 1959. The purpose of the organization had been carefully drafted, as follows:

> The purpose of this organization shall be to provide a central agency through which the efforts and activities of member units may be coordinated to more effectively promote mountain safety education, and to provide integrated mountain rescue service, to promote the free exchange of mountain rescue techniques and procedures, to disseminate advances in equipment and to promote standardization thereof as much as is possible.

The full text of the 1959 constitution can be found in Appendix C.

Signing the first constitution were delegates of the nine founding teams, plus two governmental organizations as ex-officio members. They signed in the following order:

Tacoma Mountain Rescue Unit	Lester Robinson
Corvallis Unit, Oregon Mountain Rescue	Willi Unsoeld
Portland Unit, Oregon Mountain Rescue	Richard R. Pooley

Olympic Mountain Rescue	Roy O. Harniss
Everett Mountain Rescue Unit	Ken Carpenter
Crag Rats Unit, Oregon Mountain Rescue	John W. Arens
Mountain Rescue Council, Seattle	Ome Daiber
Alpinees of Hood River, Oregon	Jack Baldwin
Seattle Air Land Emergency Team	Elmer A. Ball
Salem Unit Oregon Mountain Rescue	Thomas W. Giles
Paine Air Force Base Search and Rescue	Henry Chamberlain

An account of the formation of the MRA was published in the Seattle Mountain Rescue Council newsletter on October 6, 1959:

> The 1959 spring training conference, held at Timberline Lodge, Oregon, was an outstanding success. Not only did well over 400 people attend, but also it was the best-planned and run conference to date. A terrific amount of work went into this conference, and Oregon is certainly to be congratulated. I hope that future conferences will not be followed by actual rescues, planned or otherwise. It was interesting to note that one hundred seventy-seven from Washington attended, which does not include fifty Seattle Explorer Scouts; six came from California; one from Montana and one from Alberta, Canada. Oregon, of course, had a wonderful showing with one hundred fifty eight. This is a record to shoot at for next year. Washington will have to get on the ball to equal it.
>
> The highlight of the conference was the creation of the Mountain Rescue Association. While it is still an infant, it will grow and become a dream realized if we will put forth the effort and keep it growing. What it is and what it will become depend on what we put into it. It is important that we are no longer a scattered group of organizations unable to join together to help each other. State and national rescue organizations now have a single organization to meet instead of having to deal with each unit individually. It is fitting that Dick Pooley was elected the first president; he is a good man who will do a good job. Our own Dorrell Looff was elected vice president.

During the first years of its operation, MRA delegates met at least twice a year. Dick Pooley kept detailed records and minutes of these meetings for twenty years. Reflecting the fact that it had become a national organization, meetings were sometimes held outside the Pacific

The first four Mountain Rescue Association presidents, in front of a Seattle
Mountain Rescue Council Truck in 1965. From left: Dick Pooley, Dorrell Looff,
Don Arens, and Vance Yost.   Photo courtesy of Dick Pooley

Northwest. In 1962, the summer meeting was held in Boise, Idaho, and
in 1963, Squaw Valley, California. In 1965, the winter meeting was held
in Tucson, Arizona. The delegates returned to Squaw Valley in 1966. The
1967 and 1968 MRA meetings were held in Estes Park, Colorado and
Yosemite, California, respectively. The founding of the MRA gave
mountain rescuers a platform with which to coordinate and improve
their service to the public. The MRA eventually expanded to include
more than ninety volunteer teams from all over the United States. The
current list of member teams, as well as an overview of the MRA, can be
found at www.mra.org.

What Drives Mountain Rescuers?

Beginning with early mountaineering tragedies, this book has been an
attempt to follow the evolution of response to accidents in the
mountains by guides, park rangers and other climbers. Although the
records are often incomplete, it is clear that a new class of mountaineers
took up the call to search for and rescue fellow climbers. This leads to
the question that is a theme of this book: Who are the rescuers, and

what drives them to give their time and energy and risk their lives to
help others?

Mountain rescuers are people who have always cared about the
welfare of their fellow human beings. Many start out in scouting or
church groups dedicated to helping neighbors. Many members of these
groups carry their altruism on into their adult lives. Some learn and
develop their skills and enthusiasm as adults in other purviews, such as
the armed forces. Both groups then serve as leaders of civic activities,
where they find satisfaction in doing good deeds without tangible
rewards or recognition.

It has frequently been noted that once they are called into a search-
and-rescue situation, climbers experience an adrenalin-producing
motivation, not unlike that produced when exploring a new route up a
glacier, icefall, ridge, or wall. That adrenalin rush, the satisfaction
derived from the altruism of the endeavor, and the realization that the
people responding would also be there to help you if an accident should
happen, make search-and-rescue volunteerism an intense and satisfying
experience.

Dr. Christopher Van Tilburg of Hood River offers the following
observations in *Mountain Rescue Doctor* (2007):

> Unlike most volunteer groups, except for firefighters, we need
> to be available 24/7 for a mission. Often we know very little about
> the patient, the location, and the situation. It might be life or
> death, or it might be to escort someone out of the woods. A "head
> injury up Eagle Creek" can turn out to be an ankle sprain up
> Ruckel Creek. A "heart attack at Elk Meadows" can be an
> uninjured but stranded hiker in Newton Creek Canyon. We leave
> work, household projects, dinner parties, a warm bed, and family
> with no advance notice and precious little time to spare.
> Individually, we desire to be mountain rescuers for many reasons.
> It is a community service, we build up a good karma, we might
> need help [ourselves] one day. The camaraderie is different from
> the other aspects of our lives; here are brought together a common,
> specific task that few can complete, that is often performed under
> tense circumstances, and that usually has unpredictable obstacles.
> Highly specialized, dangerous, physically demanding, mentally
> exhausting life-or-death missions are intensely powerful stimuli.
> We gain deep satisfaction when applying our skill and knowledge

of the mountains, forests, and rivers to help those in need. We thrive on the adventure—the adrenaline rush begins with the call-out page and doesn't dissipate until the mission is completed. The thrill is compelling, the danger alluring, and the personal gratification is hedonistic. It is a pure, unadulterated form of pleasure. Altruism has its rewards, too, otherwise it would be tough to roll out of bed for the next call-out.

Some additional views:

Wolf Bauer, founder of the Seattle Mountain Rescue Council:

> As mountaineers, we always have to be concerned about safety, and there is a natural response to help each other in times of trouble. This is what got me interested and caused me to look to what they were doing in Europe; they were years ahead of us in the United States in terms of organized mountain rescue. So I brought back the Wastl Mariner rescue book and the motion picture from Munich to Seattle in 1947, and the rest is history.

Dick Pooley, first MRA president:

> Why do we do it? That is an easy question to answer, because we are all climbers, and when we hear of someone in trouble we have to respond, because we have all been there. Even If you don't know the individual personally, you get the feeling that you need to respond to a wounded buddy. As far as searching for lost people, it is a similar motivation for us, and for searches we made great use of people like Explorer Search and Rescue to help out.

Fran Sharp, MRA president 2006–2008, past president Tacoma Mountain Rescue:

> I suppose there is something in all of us that makes us want to be "the hero" in a rescue, but participation in mountain rescue is much more than that. Hours of training and preparation require some real dedication, and I believe it is more than just ego, it is about compassion. I have seen the toughest guys brought to tears when there is an outcome that is less than we had been hoping and working for. On the other hand, there is no better feeling than seeing a child reunited with a parent after a difficult search. So I believe that compassion is the driving factor behind what we do as mountain rescuers.

Rocky Henderson, MRA past president, Portland Mountain Rescue past president:

> There are lots of reasons we do what we do as volunteers, but the rewards are phenomenal. If you are involved in a mountain rescue team, you can have the opportunity to give someone their life back, and that is truly a life-changing event for the rescuer. For many of us, the feeling you get is like a drug that drives you to feel it again. I guess we all have a desire to serve the public and improve the conditions for mountain rescue, to make it a better organization. For me, my work with the MRA and my local team, Portland Mountain Rescue, is about sharing skills and mentoring the new people who come into the organization. That is the hidden reward that motivates us when the call comes in at 3 A.M.

Rick Lorenz, San Diego Mountain Rescue past president, Vice-Chair Olympic Mountain Rescue:

> When I first became involved in mountain rescue twenty years ago in California, I was on active duty in the Marine Corps. For me, the opportunity to train and participate with a volunteer civilian team was like a military reserve in reverse, and I had the chance to interact with a fine group of dedicated people in the local community. Mountain rescue brings together some wonderful opportunities, to get into the mountains with a highly capable group of people, and to be training and working on "real world" emergencies rather than purely recreational endeavors. Two recent rescues in the Olympic Mountains of Washington have been some of the most rewarding experiences of my life.

This basic issue was discussed at the very first meetings of the MRA. Here is an excerpt from the minutes of the Ad-Hoc Committee meeting in Olympia, Washington, on February 15, 1959:

> Because of some unrest regarding what appeared to be a difference of opinion of the fundamental ideas of mountain rescue, Dorrell Looff asked members in attendance to give their personal opinions why they joined mountain rescue. The result of this showed that all members were basically interested in saving lives in any manner whatsoever, and that this thought was paramount above all other reasons for joining mountain rescue.

Perhaps the best response is from Ome Daiber, founder of Seattle Mountain Rescue Council:

> It isn't that we don't care. We are there because we *do* care.

Clothing, Equipment and Technology

As I glance through the photo albums and slides from my travels in the hills, I'm most interested in the differences between the mountaineering clothing and gear of the past and that of the present. For a few years after World War II, veterans and outdoors folks were visiting Army surplus stores and acquiring collections of climbing clothing and equipment. There were roomy combat jackets and "suitcase trousers" made of tough, long-lasting fabric (with their large pockets on the thighs) that I used on Mount Rainier and during the 1953 K2 expedition. The two-man nylon tents, white on the inside and olive drab on the outside, served us well on the 1946 Mount St. Elias expedition. And, during my climbs of Rainier, I used tubular-framed rucksacks that, when overloaded, dug deeply into my hips and kidneys.

But all that has changed through the creativity of mountaineers and rescuers. We now have improved nylon ropes and web gear, and all shapes of carabiners, hammers and axes. Pitons have been mostly replaced by chockstones such as nuts and hexes, and camming devices such as "friends" for anchoring weight, and there are bat tents that can be used on vertical walls. Lightweight, warm, waterproof, moisture-wicking clothing made of abrasion-resistant materials helps rescuers deal with the elements.

In North America, mountain rescue systems have been greatly improved, and to some extent standardized, through the efforts of organizations such as Rigging for Rescue in Invermere, British Columbia, which offers training programs in equipment use. MRA team members, who already have the fundamentals, can attend such trainings and then return to their home units to train others in advanced techniques and systems.

More efficient radio communication has been facilitated by advancements in electronics. Hand-held GPS receivers can help victims pinpoint their location in the hills, and avalanche beacons can help rescuers find victims that have been buried in a snow slide. Dr. Christopher Van Tilburg (2007) echoes the concerns of many rescuers when he says, "mandating the use of an emergency-signaling device may give [people] a false sense of security—that they can climb higher and farther in bad conditions, knowing they have a fail-safe."

In 2008, there was significant controversy concerning various electronic devices that can be used in the mountains in an emergency. All rescue teams have been involved in rescues of individuals with cell phones who were otherwise ill-equipped for wilderness travel. Personal locator beacons use satellite technology to notify emergency responders of a victim's location. A commercial company has developed yet another popular emergency device that will track individuals and send emergency notification when used as part of a subscription service. Without endorsing any particular technology, the MRA monitors these developments and assists in providing accurate information about them to the MRA membership and the public.

But it all boils down to prevention and education; learning how to travel safely in the hills under all weather conditions and over all types of terrain. This has been a theme of organized mountain rescue from the beginning. Today, the MRA devotes a major part of its efforts to safety and education (more information is available at *www.mra.org*).

Chapter 8 of this book includes a section on the early history of radio communications in mountain rescue. Maintaining and improving communications between teams, and between rescuers and public officials, has always been a major objective of the MRA. This is something that can only be done by an organization that represents the interest of mountain rescuers nationally. The MRA licenses with the Federal Communications Commission (FCC) a common VHF channel (155.160 MHz) for use by all MRA teams.

The following paragraphs about radio use today were submitted by Bill Laxson, the 2009 MRA communications chairman.

Early in the twenty-first century, the FCC initiated a nationwide program to increase the number of radio channels available for use in the VHF and UHF land mobile radio frequency spectrum. This was in response to demand for ever-increasing numbers of radio channels and services. This initiative came to be known by the moniker *spectrum refarming*. Radio channels that once occupied 50 KHz of spectrum in the 1950s, and that had been split once into 25 KHz channels in the 1960s in the original "narrow-banding initiative," were again to be split into 12.5 KHz channels in the first decade of the century, and then again later into

6.25 KHz channels. The national MRA license, now with the call sign WPUA365, currently has authorizations for both legacy 25 KHz channels and the new 12.5 KHz channels.

At the end of 2008, half of the MRA units in the country had modified their licenses to accommodate the new channel split, which will become mandatory in the next few years. The spectrum that once supported only eight hundred discrete channels (among all private, state, and federal users) now supports as many as thirty-five hundred channels. In the future, the same spectrum might support seven thousand channels using yet-to-be developed technology. Currently, only a few highly proprietary radios are available that can operate at this narrow bandwidth.

Ironically, in many parts of the country, demand for land mobile radio channels has ebbed in the past few years as companies shift their internal communications from local-area two-way radio systems to the feature-rich and ubiquitous cellular systems that now offer third-generation features such as internet access, cell phone geolocation, and nationwide press-to-talk communications coverage. And a new 700 MHz spectrum providing thousands of channels is being redirected by the FCC from analog television services to public safety agencies for use in next-generation public safety communication systems.

As these agencies migrate to these new channels, widespread public demand for the legacy VHF channel 155.160 MHz coveted by mountain rescue teams will fall, making this channel and others like it more available for use by MRA teams. For although rescuers embrace and make use of these new communication technologies at times, VHF hand-held two-way radios still form the backbone of rescue communications for most teams in mountainous back-country terrain, where other communication alternatives (such as cell phones) often do not work well, and sometimes do not work at all.

MRA Missions: Who Controls and Who Pays?

In recent years, the obligation of government agencies to engage in search-and-rescue missions has often been discussed in mountaineering and governmental circles. Some members of the general public don't feel their taxes should be used to pay for the rescue of "some damned fool mountain climber." And, there have been cases in which a rescue victim or a deceased victim's family has leveled a lawsuit against the rescue agency for alleged misconduct during the rescue, causing further damage or death. At the time of this writing, none of these lawsuits has ever been successful against a volunteer rescuer. In most states, a "Good Samaritan Law" protects MRA personnel.

MRA members have long opposed "cost recovery" from the subjects of search-and-rescue missions anywhere in the country. One major concern is that these missions can be quite expensive, and people might be reluctant to call for help if they believed they would have to pay. In certain U.S. National Parks, such as Denali and Rainier, the expense of rescue is covered by the cost of the required climbing permit. In most other cases, the cost is absorbed by the local jurisdiction, and not passed on to the victim.

Regarding the ethics of mountain rescue, my eyes were opened by *Mountain Rescue Doctor: Wilderness Medicine in the Extremes of Nature* (2007) by Dr. Christopher Van Tilburg, who served in mountain rescue as a physician for many years. The book goes deeply into the ethics of mountaineering and mountain rescue work, and the bibliography of this book lists a number of volumes that cover the subject in greater detail.

Accident Reports and Safety Concerns

A perusal of The American Alpine Club's annual accident reports from 1951 and 1954–65 reveals a consistent increase in the number and seriousness of mountaineering accidents during this period. Most of these accidents were due to inexperience. This is obviously the result of the increasing interest in mountaineering, backpacking, and other outdoor sports.

The 1948 issue of *The American Alpine Journal* contains the first mention of the club's safety committee. During its first year, the committee was chaired by Bill House, a member of the 1938 American attempt on K2. The "House Chimney" on this peak was named for Bill, because of his pioneering climb up the steep cleft.

In 1949, the Safety Committee was chaired by Tacoma mountaineer Maynard Miller, who at nineteen, in 1940, was the youngest member of The American Alpine Club. In the first publication of the safety committee in 1951, Miller tabulated the estimated number of mountaineers in North America to be nearly forty thousand. The actual number was no doubt much higher, since most climbers do not join formal organizations.

The 1954 report, which came on the heels of the first ascents of several 8,000-meter peaks (Annapurna in 1950, Mount Everest in 1953, and K2 and Nanga Parbat in 1954), shows a sharp increase in public acceptance of mountaineering as a legitimate pursuit. More novices wanted to climb, and club membership increased dramatically. And in the Northwest United States, The Mountaineers and Mazamas clubs had already established classes in the techniques of safe and enjoyable climbing. The 1955 report was the first to include tabular material that listed accidents and their causes. And there was an improvement in response to an accident questionnaire sent to all the clubs. It is noteworthy that several of the accident victims of the 1950s were climbers who later gained fame in subsequent expeditions to Alaska and the Himalayas.

According to the 1956 report, the use of hardhats in rock climbing came into vogue, and greater emphasis was put on the proper use of crampons during descent. Poorly controlled glissading was listed as a common cause of falls into rocks and crevasses. Another point of emphasis was the need for experienced leaders—those who had the necessary judgment and skills to take novices into the hills. By 1957, the reports of The American Alpine Club's Accident and Safety Committee, chaired by Dr. Ben Ferris, had become popular reading material among climbers of all levels of experience.

Over the next decade, the annual accident reports covered such topics as the increase in winter mountaineering. It was at this point that hypothermia was discussed in the reports, which described problems resulting from such things as heat loss through uncovered heads, and from clothing and sleeping bags that hadn't been dried out completely. The topic of rope strength brought about the testing of ropes for tensile strength and elasticity. Some deaths caused by lightning demonstrated the importance of getting off the peaks before afternoon thunderstorms, especially when carrying metal items. Reports about suffocation inside tents during storms emphasized the need to maintain air circulation in confined spaces.

In 1962, the club's report included information on climbing accidents in Canada. It was found that more accidents occurred on snow and ice than on other terrain. Also, more victims were older Americans, possibly due to their ability to travel farther from home to do their mountaineering. Information on the tabulation of accidents became more standardized. It was found that uncontrolled glissading by inexperienced climbers had become the primary cause of slips and falls into rocks and crevasses. By then, hardhats had become standard equipment, and studies were made of their design to better protect the head. It was also determined that accidents while rappelling were often the result of a lack of training and experience, and sometimes of carelessness on the part of experienced climbers when they were setting up belay points.

In 1963, the report discussed the revised edition of Wastl Mariner's Austrian "bible" of mountain search-and-rescue techniques. The 1964 report covered a discussion of frostbite and the various types of mountaineering boots. And, in 1966, a discussion of "club" expeditions brought out the possible negative consequences of previously unacquainted people meeting for the first time after the expedition had begun. It discussed common problems within such teams, such as inexperience, incompatibility, and varying quality of clothing and equipment.

The American Alpine Club accident reports (*Accidents in North American Mountaineering*) have become popular instruction books, and are the basis for better understanding and evaluation of the causes of mishaps in the mountains.

The MRA Today and Tomorrow

The rest of the early history of the Mountain Rescue Association remains to be written; this is a small but prominent slice of that history. The teams outside the Pacific Northwest that helped found and form the MRA in its early years, and the stories of those and more recent MRA teams throughout the United States and Canada, and even in a few other countries, remain to be published in book form. For now, let us fast forward to what the MRA has evolved into, what it is faced with today, and what it aspires to in the future.

The MRA has reached maturity and is now the principal organization dealing with people in distress in the mountains, with more than ninety teams and two thousand members in the United States and Canada. Most of the members are volunteers, or more accurately unpaid professional experts, who work through local government search-and-rescue authority. In many cases, they are the sole providers of mountain search and rescue in their areas. In an effort to give back to the community, defray public agency costs and keep taxes down, MRA teams have been performing the bulk of all mountain search-and-rescue missions in the U.S. and Canada for the past fifty years without any charge to the subject.

Fifty years have passed since the founding of the MRA, but there is still no government funding and taxing sufficient to pay for this 24-hours-a-day, 7-days-a-week, 365-days-a-year life-saving service. MRA members remain the primary providers of mountain search and rescue in the United States, and they gladly and with passion donate hours and professional-level expertise to their communities that rival any full-time career.

Volunteer mountain rescuers come from all walks of life. They share an interest in climbing and mountaineering with their teammates and give selflessly of their time to keep themselves proficient in mountain skills, both individual and rescue-specific. The organization and complexity of mission planning might have changed, but the enthusiasm and commitment of MRA members is the same today as it was when the MRA was founded in 1959.

Mountain rescue and the operation of mountain rescue teams require people with a great variety of administrative and practical skills. Included are those with experience in promotion and fund-raising, those who specialize in the design of equipment for the rescue and transport of victims to trailheads and helicopter landing areas, those who find the ultimate in mountaineering challenges to be the overcoming of obstacles such as inclement weather and difficult terrain, and those who keep track of the economic aspects of rescue missions. There are also the writers and publicists who report rescue details, and statisticians who record the trends. Lastly, there are the legal experts who see that everything is conducted within the constraints of local laws and regulations.

The MRA focuses on training and education as the keystones of mountain safety. This is part of the principle that every individual who heads into the outdoors must accept responsibility for his or her actions, and that having training in basic outdoor skills and self-rescue is the best way of resolving mountain emergencies. The MRA maintains stringent requirements for teams to join. Each member team must pass three tests, each based on guidelines established by the association. Each team is certified by the evaluators in the three major areas of high-angle rock rescue, ice and snow rescue, and wilderness search.

Once a team achieves full MRA status, new members are trained to MRA standards and tested by their team. MRA-qualified personnel within the teams are called rescue members and are authorized to wear the blue and white MRA logo. These members have worked hard to maintain their qualifications, both at the individual and team level, and to develop a high level of pride and teamwork.

Some new challenges facing the MRA in 2009

At recent national meetings of the Mountain Rescue Association, a recurrent topic for discussion and action is the federal National Incident Management System standards and how they are likely to be applied to volunteer teams throughout the United States. NIMS was created after the 9/11 terrorist attacks in New York and Washington in 2001, and is now a key part of the national search-and-rescue system. Homeland Security Presidential Directive 5, "Management of Domestic Incidents," requires the adoption of the NIMS standards by all levels of government. Federal preparedness assistance funding for states, local jurisdictions and tribal entities is now dependent on NIMS compliance. At the January 2006 MRA meeting in Salt Lake City, there was a general consensus that the "train is coming down the track" and that local MRA teams should be prepared to deal with the new standards.

The impact of this can be seen in the state of Washington, home to six MRA teams. Search and rescue in Washington is governed primarily by state law, which defines search and rescue, assigns responsibilities, and establishes the position and duties of the state Coordinator for SAR Operations. It also establishes the extensive liability protection and compensation program which protects search-and-rescue volunteers in the state. This includes the "Good Samaritan" law which helps to protect volunteers and state workers from lawsuits.

The responsibility for search and rescue rests with the "local chief law enforcement officer" (usually the county sheriff). Local directors of emergency management coordinate support for search-and-rescue operations in their jurisdictions and must register volunteers in accordance with state law. The state SAR Coordinator is responsible for resource coordination, multi-jurisdiction operations coordination, and administration of the Emergency Worker Program.

Standards for Mountain Rescue

Creating acceptable and formalized standards for rescuers has proven to be a controversial subject. The problem is to develop standards that are adequate, but not unduly restrictive. Also, setting requirements that can later become the basis for lawsuits when not followed is problematic. The process to develop standards is now driven by federal law, and the availability of federal funds to local jurisdictions.

In NIMS standards, there is an important difference between "typing" (characterization), which applies to teams or units, and "credentialing," which applies to individual responders. Typing has already occurred, although it has not yet had much practical impact on volunteer teams in the state of Washington. You can see the results and the Federal Emergency Management Agency (FEMA) standards for four types of teams at http://www.nimsonline.com/resource_typing/Wilderness%20Search%20and%20Rescue%20Team.htm.

For example, a "Type I" Wilderness Search and Rescue Team should have forty-eight members and six team leaders and be capable of conducting self-sustained field operations for seventy-two hours. Type II and III teams would have lower qualifications, and, presumably, each team would be employed only according to its qualifications.

The process of credentialing and standards development for mountain rescue personnel is ongoing at the Federal level. The MRA has a representative on the FEMA working group that is tasked with making recommendations for revisions of the requirements. These are considered by the U.S. Department of Homeland Security to be living documents—ongoing projects. In January of 2006, the MRA adopted new policy guidelines for teams wishing to have their members meet the NIMS standards. This has become a topic of discussion in every MRA team, and most of them have already made the decision to comply, based upon requirements placed by their local law enforcement agencies. This has been difficult for many long-time MRA volunteers to accept, but it is slowly becoming a reality for all teams.

With the ability of the MRA to have direct input in the form of a working group member into the development of the federal standards for mountain search and rescue, the resulting documents stand a chance of being useable by the existing rescue teams as well as being effective in the manner in which they were intended by the federal government. Work on these standards will continue for many years to come.

Federal regulation is having a major impact on all MRA teams. Gone are the days when a few climbing buddies went out on their own initiative or responded to a call for help from the family of a missing climber or hiker. We can be nostalgic about the good old days when individual courage and skills ruled mountains, but today, we have to rely on the authority legally responsible for search and rescue, and we have to talk the NIMS language. This is the only way for volunteer mountain-rescue teams to coordinate effectively with local authorities, and operate responsibly in the field.

The Big Picture

The reader might wonder how the MRA fits in with other search-and-rescue teams that are not MRA members. It would perhaps be elitist to simply touch on the current times without acknowledging the MRA's place among other search-and-rescue assets. The MRA has many brother and sister teams in the country that perform search, flat-land rescue, technical rope rescue, urban search-and-rescue, and more, and there are brother and sister national associations for search and rescue teams of that nature. The MRA's unique specialty is in mountain search and rescue, including high-angle and technical rope rescue and snow and ice rescue. It is in this area that MRA teams excel and are particularly qualified. Just as it was in the early days of mountain rescue, the MRA to this day still brings that unique specialty and expertise "to the table" of the search-and-rescue response system in the United States and beyond.

Today, the dedicated volunteer members of the Mountain Rescue Association perform valuable services to the public with little fanfare or expectation of reward. The MRA owes a great debt to its founding members, who had the foresight to lay the framework for the MRA of today. Technology and conditions have changed over the years, but the commitment is fundamentally the same: "The mountains don't care, but *we* do!"

Afterword

A Thought for Weary Old Rescuers

"There are many stories you may hear, in response to leading questions, regarding the effect of these regions [the Canadian Rockies] on different men. There was a prospector, incapacitated by age and infirmities, who used to sit by the hour on the veranda of his valley home looking up at the ranges. Once or twice, he tried to go back again and, too old, fell by the trail, where searchers found him and packed him home again. The neighbors began to talk of sending him to the Old Man's Home, and he overheard. One day he disappeared. No one knew where he had gone. At last, an Indian was found who had seen him. A search party went out, picked up his trail, and followed it. It led into a majestic basin of the high country.

There they found the old man lying dead, and around him were explanatory marks. He had been running and leaping, leaping many feet. The general view was that talk of the Old Man's Home had been too much for that aged old man of the mountains, and that he had crept up there and then deliberately, knowing what would be the result to his weak heart, had run and leapt and run again and so fallen at last dead in the world he loved, the high country cliffs looking blankly down on him."

FREDERICK NIVENS (1962)

Appendixes

Selected Mountain Rescue Leadership in Washington

> *The leader of any expedition should be the member who has the greatest experience and knowledge combined with sound judgment and an ability to command respect.*
>
> THE AMERICAN ALPINE CLUB (1956)

Traditionally, individual members of search and rescue teams choose to remain anonymous. We exist under the name of our team; individual publicity is generally beyond our operating philosophy. Although some might object, here are a few lines about the backgrounds of some of the more dedicated and long-serving Washington search-and-rescue leaders. Appendix B contains information about some of the individuals of that same caliber who were leaders in Oregon.

Two individuals that I consider the most significant early rescuers on Mount Rainier head the list. We apologize in advance to rescuers that were not mentioned or received less coverage than they deserve in this volume. It is hoped that this book will motivate others to write more about the people who had an important role in mountain rescue.

Photo from the Dee
Molenaar Collection

Charlie Browne

Charlie Browne, who led the teams that retrieved the bodies of Forrest Greathouse and Edwin Wetzel from crevasses on Mount Rainier in 1929, served in the National Park Service from the 1920s through the 1950s. As a result of his rescue efforts, he earned a special citation for heroism from the Department of the Interior. I believe that while he worked at Rainier, he occupied the small log cabin inside the Nisqually entrance. He then served at Olympic National Monument, before it became a national park in 1938. He was a hardy, impish man with a warm sense of humor. He had his own home in Port Angeles, from where he enjoyed fishing and golfing. I recall first meeting Charlie during one of the ranger indoctrination and training sessions at Longmire early in the summer of 1948. I later visited him in Port Angeles.

Photo by the author

William Jackson "Bill" Butler

Assistant Chief Ranger Bill Butler at Mount Rainier was known as one who was there wherever and whenever help was needed on "The Mountain" from the 1930s through the 1960s. Born in Tennessee in 1909, Bill became acquainted with Mount Rainier in 1929, when, while hitchhiking through the Northwest en route to Alaska, he heard of a big rescue operation on the mountain. He decided to alter his course, and walked all the way from Tacoma to the park. He eventually worked as a guide for a few years before beginning his career in the National Park Service in 1936.

During World War II, Bill served with the U.S. Army in Europe, and then returned to Mount Rainier. During my brief tenure in the Park Service at Rainier, I enjoyed sharing many "business" trips with Bill. These included several mountain search-and-rescue operations, patrols of the rope-tow equipped ski slopes at Paradise, one winter at Canyon Rim, and wintry ski searches for and repairs of downed power and phone lines between Paradise, Longmire, and the park entrance.

Bill had many opportunities for advancement within the Park Service, but, as they all required transfers to other parks, he declined, preferring to remain on the mountain he loved. For his many search-and-rescue missions at Mount Rainier, Bill became the honored subject of an episode of the popular TV program "This Is Your Life," hosted by Ralph Edwards.

With his wife, "Marthie," whom he had met at the park in the 1930s, Bill eventually retired, after forty years of service, to a home overlooking Puget Sound near Olympia. After a few years there, he survived Marthie's passing from cancer, and, later, the passing of his second wife, Audrey, who was Marthie's cousin. He always helped his neighbors if they were in trouble. Bill's nearly annual elk-hunting pilgrimages and

occasional recreational skiing trips had to be curtailed somewhat when
he suffered a knee injury while trimming tree branches.

Sadly, in 1993, Bill suffered physical problems that resulted in his
living with and being cared for by a family friend, Sonya Wallick. His
situation deteriorated, and he had to be placed in a retirement home in
Tumwater. This situation was emotionally tough on Bill, whose life had
been devoted to caring for other people. During my last visit with Bill
in April 1995, it was apparent he was suffering the early stages of
Alzheimer's disease. He passed away in 2000.

Early Leaders of the Seattle Mountain Rescue Council

Ome Daiber

A 2002 article by Lowell Skoog, historian for The
Mountaineers, provided information about Ome
Daiber's early life.

Photo from the Dee
Molenaar Collection

Ome Daiber was born George C. Daiber in 1907, and
later changed his name legally to Ome. The name Ome
is from his boyhood, when he asked a friend at school to "owe me a
nickel" so he could buy some lunch.

Ome's daughter Joanne recalled an early climbing story about her
father. "One of Ome's first conquests was the roof of his house. He
climbed up the down-spout." His wife, Matie, remembered that "his
mother almost fainted when she saw him." Joanne continued, "He
climbed up the down-spout somehow and then he did a swing. He had
one hand on the gutter and one hand on the down-spout and he did a
swing and up and over as his mother came around the corner, and she
screamed as he was going—you know, the best thing for a mother to do."

Ome ran Ome Daiber, Inc., making and selling equipment. One of
Ome's early inventions was the Penguin sleeping bag, which enabled the
user to "get up without getting out of bed." Matie recalled that Ome
started making Penguins early in the 1930s, and they were featured in the
film "Mountains Don't Care" in 1953 by Ira Spring. Other Ome Daiber
inventions included Bird Cage crampons (lightweight, made of round
metal stock welded together), the Pac-Jacket, and Sno-Seal. Mountaineers
in the Northwest were glopping Sno-Seal on their leather boots for many
years until it was replaced by high-tech waterproofing material.

When Delmar Fadden was lost on Mount Rainier in the winter of 1936, the authorities called Ome for help because of his Rainier experience; he made a first ascent of Liberty Ridge the previous September. As a result of this rescue operation, Ome became the go-to man for mountain rescues for many years thereafter. Calls would come to the Daiber house, then Matie and Ome would call a list of their mountaineering friends to help. Ome was therefore a key player when the Seattle Mountain Rescue Council was founded in 1948.

Dr. Otto Trott offered his thoughts about Ome in a letter shortly after Ome's death in 1989.

Ome Daiber had only friends; he had no enemies. His outstanding leadership qualities often created some controversy, but every disagreement ended on a positive note, because it soon became evident that the basic principle behind Ome's opinions and decisions was his altruism— his overwhelming desire to help others who were in need of help. Nothing could stand in his way when he felt that there was such a need.

His philosophy made him a natural leader. The Seattle Mountain Rescue Council was created by engineer Wolf Bauer, who called people together who were interested in mountaineering. While he worked on the organization phase, he designated Ome as the rescue leader in the field and Dr. Otto Trott as the medical advisor. This newly formed council created among them a lasting, cooperative friendship. Of course, many other friends of Ome and Wolf were involved in the formation of, or later participated in, this newly created concept. It would be difficult to name all of them, but there were many, and every one made his or her inimitable contribution to the total program.

Ome Daiber was a person nobody could ever forget, a small, almost ascetic-looking man who moved quickly and decisively. When Ome lectured to different audiences, often with Otto supplying supporting words about the medical aspects of mountain rescue, he could belabor details in an agonizingly slow way. Even so, his great sense of humor always endeared him to his audience. His fame grew as the best person to be contacted to immediately initiate the rescue of a climber or downed plane pilot. He had earned his reputation long before Wolf Bauer created the SMRC.

Ome well understood other people's feelings and their abilities, which enabled him to maintain lasting cooperation with the many agencies with whom he worked: police, sheriffs, the Washington State Patrol,

Army, Navy, and Coast Guard. They were all convinced of his sincerity, kindness, and intense desire to be helpful. Ome never expressed any disrespect for their authority; he was an excellent diplomat.

Ome came across as friendly and sharp as a tack, a little guy who greeted new friends with a warm smile and the phrase, "I'm Ome Daiber and I don't like you either." There was always a warm feeling of accomplishment in each rescue, and a strong fellowship developed between rescuers. Over the years, as better rescue equipment was developed, much of it by Ome, and as his experience in mountain rescue grew, Ome formed a philosophy that carried him through even the grimmest circumstances. Ome's own words probably say it best: "When we go out on a mission, we simply do what we need to do. It's not fun, but we have to do it. We go out on a rescue mission hoping to save a life. Sometimes we get there too late; the life has already been taken. Then we do what we have to do. And while we are on a mission, from the point of the pick-up down to the road, we have a hilarious time. It's the only way we can handle it."

Through his climbing and mountain-rescue work, Ome patented numerous inventions. And his inventiveness, underlying his many patents, saved the day on a number of climbs and rescues in the mountains. As he once commented, "When anybody says it can't be done, suddenly I become totally deaf. If mortal man made it, mortal man can fix it."

OME DAIBER'S CODE FOR MOUNTAIN RESCUES

1. When someone is lost or in distress, we go.

2. The only questions are: Can it be done? How? With what equipment? By whom? and How soon?

3. Potential rescuers must be ready to go for anyone.

4. We have no concern for the individual's money or the lack of it, race, religion, national origin, amount of education, name, or status.

5. Some won't go if a victim is a hunter, or for some other reason, or would only go for certain people. We go for anyone in trouble regardless of his reason for being in the wilderness.

6. We don't stop to question the recklessness of the climber, or foolishness, or downright stupidity of the act, or poor judgment that precipitated the emergency.

7. The immediate question is not what it will cost or who will pay for it.

8. The field leader has to do whatever is needed each and every moment.

9. Even if a victim is already dead, he or she will be retrieved if at all possible.

Wolf Bauer

Photo courtesy of Wolf Bauer

Born in Bavaria, Germany in 1912, Wolf Bauer came to Seattle in the 1925 and immediately noted that the Cascade Range is similar to that of his native Alps. With his boundless energy and vision, in 1934 he established The Mountaineers climbing course. A champion skier, he competed in the 1936 Olympic trials at Mount Rainier. In the 1940s, in the Silver Skis Races there, he skied the four mile race from 10,000-foot Camp Muir to 5,400-foot Paradise Valley. When he returned from a trip to his native Germany in 1947, he brought with him the mountain rescue manual and motion picture that would mark the beginning of organized mountain rescue in the United States. In 1948, he established both the Washington Kayak Club and the Seattle Mountain Rescue Council.

A graduate of the University of Washington, with a degree combining Geology and Ceramic Engineering, Wolf generously helped establish ceramic plants in third world countries around the world. He is also a consulting authority in the control of stream and shoreline features through the design of structures that decrease erosion and increase deposition to enhance the local fishery habitats.

A chronology of Wolf Bauer's life reads like a "Who's Who" of contributors to outdoor recreation and wilderness conservation. In 1933, Wolf obtained permission from the Seattle Area Boy Scout Council to offer Explorer Scouts basic mountaineering instruction. He also took them to a glacial boulder to practice climbing. This instruction resulted in the formation of the Ptarmigan Climbing Club some years later by a group of the former scouts. The Ptarmigan club made its mark exploring the North Cascades. During the 1940s and 1950s, he made the first foldboat descents of several Northwest rivers. In 1948, with Ome Daiber and Dr. Otto Trott, he founded the Seattle Mountain Rescue Council. In 1952, with Jack Hossack, he developed the Stokeski rescue stretcher. In 1959, at Mount Hood, he was among those who formed the national Mountain Rescue Association. In 1966, he was made an honorary member of The Mountaineers.

In the late 1960s, Wolf directed a successful campaign to preserve the Green River Gorge, near Seattle. He was a founding member of the Washington Environmental Council in 1969. He launched, in the early 1970s, a second career as a shore-resources consultant. He was honored, in 1979, as a First Citizen of Seattle for his work to preserve the shoreline resources of Seattle. He received a Special Services Award from the Washington chapter of the American Society of Landscape Architects in 1987. And in 1991, he received an award from the Washington State Department of Ecology in recognition of his dedication and commitment to protecting shoreline resources under the Shoreline Management Act of 1971.

Photo courtesy of
Seattle Museum of
History and Industry

Dr. Otto Trott

A skier and climber since his youth in Germany, the forthright Dr. Otto Trott put patients first. He played Good Samaritan whenever he encountered an accident or illness, without fear of a lawsuit. When the going got tough, as in a gritty mountain rescue, he treated colleagues to stress-melting jokes.

"He took his work seriously," said SMRC co-founder Wolf Bauer. "But he knew when to lighten things up. He had a wonderful sense of humor." Born to art-gallery owners in Berlin, Dr. Trott earned his medical degree at the University of Freiburg in 1936. Part Jewish, he immigrated to the United States in 1937 to escape persecution.

Trott completed a residency in Syracuse, N.Y., and in 1939 he moved to Seattle to work for the King County Public Health Department. He joined Seattle's mountaineering community and became a founding member of the Ski Patrol on Mount Baker, where he kept a cabin. The mountain's "Ottobahn" run bears his name.

During World War II, not here long enough to have become a U.S. citizen, Trott was placed in a Tennessee internment camp. As camp doctor, he developed an anti-venom serum for bites from black widow spiders. He became a naturalized citizen in 1946. He returned to the Northwest to practice medicine in Seattle and enjoy mountaineering in the North Cascades, which he called "the American Alps."

With Bauer and mountaineer Ome Daiber, he created the Seattle Mountain Rescue Council that addressed rescue needs outside regular ski areas, which already were covered by the National Ski Patrol. He helped develop gear and techniques drawn from European rescue models but tailored for American conditions. He won many awards for his rescue efforts and for work with the Capitol Hill Clinic and Swedish Medical Center, in Seattle.

I recall Otto coming up to Paradise Valley on Mount Rainier, with Ome Daiber, Wolf Bauer, and Kurt Beam, to join some of us rangers in filming crevasse-rescue techniques. Famed photographer Ira Spring was there to capture our raising of a victim from a crevasse and transporting him back down the glacier via one of those waist-high, ski-equipped wire baskets. Later, during a joint Park Service-Forest Service-SMRC gathering atop the Stevens Pass Ski Area, my wife Colleen was persuaded to allow herself to be tied into a wire basket and lowered over some high cliffs.

Through their German-Austrian language expertise, Otto and Kurt Beam worked, and occasionally fought, together preparing an English version of the Wastl Mariner guide about mountain rescue techniques that Wolf Bauer brought back from a trip to Germany in 1947.

On one occasion, I was with Otto when more than fifteen of us were jammed into a five-man Army tent at Windy Corner on Mount McKinley, during our evacuation of the Whittakers off the mountain after their fall below Denali Pass. During our thirty-six hours in that wind-blasted tent, I clearly recall Otto heroically keeping the soup going on the primus stove, patiently ignoring frequent awkward moves by someone's foot that tipped over the pot.

The Trotts' cabin near the community of Glacier was always open to fellow skiers and climbers, and, in 1990, Otto offered the use of his cabin to Pete Schoening and me, along with Marcus Schmuck and Fritz Wintersteller, two of Austria's world-class climbers who, in 1959, had made the first ascent of Broad Peak in the Karakoram Range. We spent the night there after a lengthy, fog-bound, one-day climb of Mount Shuksan.

In 1956, Otto was a member of an expedition to the East Ridge of Mount McKinley that was undertaken to determine if Dr. Frederick Cook could have climbed the peak the way he claimed he did in 1906. From their experience on the mountain, they concluded that Cook could not have taken that route.

Everyone in the area involved in mountain search-and-rescue operations during his time, whether victims, rescuers, or just passive observers, will remember Dr. Otto Trott for his honesty, integrity, sense of humor (and of the ridiculous), and dedication to making the ski and mountain slopes safe and enjoyable places to seek healthful exercise and rejuvenation of the spirit. He died in 1999 of heart failure, at age eighty-eight.

Kurt Beam

Kurt Beam was born in Vienna in 1919. He came to the United States in the 1930s. Kurt was a member of the Mountain Rescue Association, National Ski Patrol, National Ski Instructors Association, The American Alpine Club, and The Mountaineers.

Photo by the author

Kurt considered as his most memorable mountaineering adventure a lightning-harassed ascent in 1950 of Mount Assiniboine in British Columbia with the famed guide Erling Strom.

An early member of the Seattle Mountain Rescue Council, Kurt participated in more than twenty alpine rescue operations in the Cascades and Olympic Mountains. With Dr. Otto Trott, he translated into English the first internationally published instruction book on mountain search-and-rescue techniques, which had been written by Wastl Mariner. As a certified professional ski instructor, he taught skiing well into his seventies. A vagabond at heart, Kurt traveled widely, often visiting Central and South America, and once making a trip to Antarctica with his wife, Ruth.

Upon his retirement and because of his abiding love of the Vienna and Salzburg areas of Austria, Kurt became a certified travel agent. He organized and led numerous skiers from Seattle on trips to ski areas in Austria. Kurt was named as an honorary representative of the Tyrolean Tourist Board, and was formally presented with an award for his contributions to the country's tourist business by the President of Austria.

It was my pleasure to have Kurt join our "old cronies expeditions." We traveled the West visiting the locales of youthful hikes, climbs, and ski trips. During our evening cocktail hours in motels along the way, we enjoyed his ribald humor and tales of his ski tours to the Old Country. He passed away in 2007.

Max Eckenburg

Photo courtesy of
Seattle Museum of
History and Industry

Max Eckenburg was born in Aberdeen, Washington in 1916, raised in logging camps and developed strong outdoor skills. He started his college education in California and made a number of first ascents in the Sierras in the early 1930s. He worked in the Civilian Conservation Corps designing trails, fighting fires, and manning lookouts, and worked for the U.S. Forest Service in the Mount Baker District. He was a draftsman for Boeing, working on the B-17 bomber during World War II. He passed away in 2001.

I first met Max in Glacier, Washington in the spring of 1946, while registering for an attempted first ascent of the Nooksack Tower on Mount Shuksan, with my brother K and Maynard Miller. After our failed attempt, we returned to Glacier a day late. We arrived just as Max and a couple of others were preparing a search party.

After several years with the Forest Service, Max took over the management of the Boy Scouts' Camp Sheppard, in the woods adjacent to Highway 410 en route to the east side of Mount Rainier. There, he organized an Explorer Scouts unit and taught the boys mountaineering and mountain rescue techniques. Eckenburg was a co-founder of Explorer Search and Rescue in 1954.

Max was also a leading figure in the construction of the Camp Schurman Stone Shelter at Steamboat Prow on Mount Rainier. This involved carrying construction materials to the site in backpacks and the construction of the cabin itself, both requiring numerous volunteers over the course of several summers.

Over the years, Max took part in a number of search-and-rescue missions in the Cascades and Olympics. He also became the subject of a mountain rescue effort on Mount Olympus when he suffered an attack of appendicitis. He barely made it out in time.

Paul Williams

Photo courtesy of the
Williams family

Paul Williams was born in Cleveland, Ohio to F. C. "Chet" and Marge Williams. He moved with his family to the Puget Sound area in 1929. He graduated from St. Anne's School and Queen Anne High School, and attended Seattle University. He served with the U.S.

Marine Corps in the Pacific from 1943 to 1946, and, upon his return, graduated from Gonzaga University Law School in Spokane in 1952.

Williams started his law career in downtown Seattle in 1952. For the next thirteen years, he practiced law in Shoreline and Edmonds, and worked as legal counsel for the Alyeska Pipeline Service Company in Fairbanks, Alaska. He satisfied his interest in the outdoors by climbing and hiking in the Northwest, Alaska, and Argentina. He climbed Mount Rainier several times, all the major peaks in Washington and Oregon, many peaks in Canada, Mount McKinley in Alaska, and Mount Popocatepetl in Mexico, and made two attempts on Mount Aconcagua in Argentina, the tallest peak in the Western hemisphere. In later years, he started hiking wilderness beaches on Vancouver Island with his longtime mountain climbing friend Bill Dougall. He wrote a book called *Oregon Coast Hikes* published by The Mountaineers Books in 1987 that covered the entire Oregon Coast. He led adventure trips for Dick McGowan of Mountain Travel that took him to Turkey, Alaska, Nepal and Canada.

Williams was active in the rescue world for nearly a half century. An avid mountain climber, in 1953 he joined the Seattle Mountain Rescue Council. He served a term as chairman, and was a well-respected base operations leader. He was also the group's legal counsel for many years.

In 1959, Paul drew up the papers that incorporated the Mountain Rescue Association (MRA), and later he served one term as its president. He was a driving force behind the decision to form the MRA and get its constitution signed. He wrote a guide titled *Rescue Leadership* that is still used by rescue groups today.

I met Paul Williams during a ski climb and descent of Mount St. Helens in the late 1950s. He took a leading role in many missions in the Cascade Range and Olympic Mountains and was among those serving in a support capacity in Talkeetna with Ome Daiber during the 1960 Mount McKinley evacuation expedition.

George Sainsbury

George Sainsbury was involved in his first mission, a search and recovery on the Oregon coast, in 1944. In 1947, he took part in the last major mission in the area before the organization of the Seattle Mountain Rescue

Photo by the author

Council, a search and recovery on Mount Index. After taking a six-week course in rescue from Wolf Bauer in 1952 and joining the SMRC, Sainsbury moved to Bremerton and was one of the founders of Olympic Mountain Rescue. George's professional career was with the Boy Scouts.

In August of 1957, George sustained a crippling injury while trying to put up a new route up the Kautz Cleaver on Mount Rainier that effectively ended his climbing career. He was in a cast for eight months and walked with a cane for two more years. Prior to that accident, he had climbed more than one hundred twenty-five peaks in the United States and Canada. In 1958, he was chosen to lead several local members of The American Alpine Club in revising the 1949 edition of *A Climber's Guide to the Cascade and Olympic Mountains of Washington* by Fred Beckey. Shortly after that, he became a member of the club's Safety Committee, on which he served for thirty-seven years.

George served as chairman of the SMRC from 1964–1966 and 1972–1975. During the forty years from 1950 to 1990, George took part in three hundred sixty rescue missions, usually as the base or in-town operations leader. George estimates that he has spent two years of his life on missions. George is past president of the Washington region of the MRA, held officer positions in the national MRA on several occasions, and was honored with a life membership in the MRA in 1992. He was one of the founders of the King County Search and Rescue Association. George served on the Board of Directors of The American Alpine Club, was the chairman of the Cascade Section of this organization, and received its Angelo Heilprin Award for his service to American mountaineering. He was also on the REI Board of Directors in the 1970s. George also contributed the chapter "Mountain Rescue" to *The Book of Modern Mountaineering* by Malcolm Milne, published in 1968.

Dorrell Looff

Photo courtesy of
Dick Pooley

Dorrell Looff was born in Seattle at Luna Park on Alki Point, in a small house attached to the amusement park. Ome Daiber would later say "Dorrell was born on a merry go-round and never got off." Looff's family soon moved to Santa Monica, California where they helped construct the Santa Monica Pier. The family returned to Seattle in 1921, and Dorrell finished high school in Seattle. He served with the U.S.

Navy in the Pacific in World War II and went on to work for
Washington Mutual for 40 years, becoming a vice president. He was one
of the founders of Seattle Mountain Rescue Council in 1948 and later
went on to be its chairman. His wife, Sally, was one of the "call girls"
who ran the call-out system for the team with Matie Daiber.

Dorrell was one of the leading figures in the establishment of the
MRA and drafting its constitution, with Paul Williams and George
Sainsbury. He was elected the second president of the MRA, and served
from 1961 to 1963. In addition to his service in the MRA he was proud
of the fact that he served as a Red Cross Volunteer for twenty-five years.

Other notables

Peter Kittlesby "Pete" Schoening

I first met Pete Schoening during the summer of 1952 at
the Paradise Ranger Station on Mount Rainier, where I
approved him for a summit climb while working as a
ranger. Then, in 1953, we began a lasting friendship while
participating in the Third American Karakoram

Photo from the Dee
Molenaar Collection

Expedition to K2, the world's second highest mountain. At age twenty-
six, Pete was the youngest member of our eight-man party, but probably
the strongest climber. Six of us ended up owing our lives to Pete because
of his strong belay, which stopped us during a fall down the upper
mountain while descending the peak in a storm with a disabled Art
Gilkey, who died later in the descent.

After his return from K2, Pete married Mary Lou "Mell" Deuter, a
childhood sweetheart, and they built a beautiful home on the shore of
Lake Washington, near Bothell.

In 1958, Schoening and Andy Kauffman were the first Americans to
make a first ascent of an 8,000-meter peak, the 26,470 foot Hidden Peak
(also known as Gasherbrum I). In 1966, he was one of Nick Clinch's
team that reached the top of the 16,100 foot Vinson Massif, the highest
point in Antarctica. He also ascended several other high summits in the
Sentinel Range.

Pete and I have made numerous climbs together in the Cascades and
Olympic Mountains, including the first ascent of the Wilson Glacier
Headwall on Mount Rainer in 1957. Into his sixties, Pete continued to

climb, ski, cycle, and canoe vigorously, and, in spite of an artificial hip, he still participated in expeditions to remote parts of China.

After retirement in 1995, Pete returned to serious mountaineering. In 1995, he climbed Aconcagua in the Andes and Kilimanjaro in Africa. In 1996, he was a member of Scott Fisher's tragedy-marred expedition to Mount Everest, but fortunately, Pete was acclimatizing at Base Camp when tragedy overtook those above. But Pete's nephew Klev Schoening successfully summited and returned, in typical Schoening fashion, carrying a sick Sherpa down the mountain.

Pete was elected an honorary member of The American Alpine Club in 1992 and The Mountaineers in 1996. In 1997, at the age of seventy-nine, I enjoyed a quick trip into the Wind Rivers with Pete and his son Eric. They climbed Gannett Peak. Unable to keep up, I ended up as base camp coordinator. This was the last in Pete's collection of the fifty states' highest points.

Photo by the author

George Senner

George Senner was born and raised in Kansas farm country. After moving to Tacoma with his folks, George became acquainted with Mount Rainier via one-day bicycling round-trips to the mountain's northwestern corner. One day, he was called to the office at Lincoln High School by a large man in a National Park Service uniform, Chief Ranger Albert Rose. He was surprised to be offered a job as fire lookout at Anvil Rock. This was George's first contact with the Park Service. At that time, there was a shortage of summer employees, with so many young men being called into military service.

Upon being drafted into the Army in 1942, George joined the 85th Mountain Infantry of the famed "Ski Troops" being trained at Camp Hale, Colorado. He served with distinction in the Italian Campaign, which helped bring the war in Europe to an end. George and I first met at the University of Washington in 1947. Except for my brother K, George was my closest and most frequent climbing companion over the years. During the summers of 1947 and 1951, we worked together as seasonal rangers at Paradise, and, as such, took part in a number of rescue missions in the park.

He met his future wife, Gloria "Glo" Olsen at Paradise, where she worked for the Rainer National Park Company as a waitress and at the soda fountain. They were married in 1948 and, upon George's graduation from the university in 1949 with a degree in geography, they left for a summer in Europe in 1951. This turned into a 4-year stint. George worked for the U.S. government in the stabilization of war-torn Germany. His initial job was managing the Schneefernerhaus atop the Zugspitze, the highest peak in Germany. He later was involved in evaluating and returning to Austrians the properties they lost during the Nazi takeover. Life in the Alps was good for George and Glo as they bicycled to numerous destinations. George later guided K and me to these same destinations during our climbing visit to the Alps in 1973.

George joined the SMRC in the early 1950s, and took part in many missions, including the Mount McKinley operation in May 1960. He was also a member of the party that made the first ascent of Mount Kennedy in 1965, with Senator Robert F. Kennedy and Everest ascender Jim Whittaker. In July of 1965, George invited me to join him in climbing Mount Rainier with Washington Governor Daniel Evans. George and Glo Senner hosted numerous gatherings of skiers and climbers at their Seattle home, which helped all of us to maintain contact.

William Francis "Willi" Unsoeld

Photo by the author

I first met Bill Unsoeld in January of 1954 (prior to his claiming the alpine moniker "Willi"), at the home of Sierra Nevada historian Francis and Marjorie Farquhar in Berkeley, California. The occasion was the showing of my K2 slides to members of the forthcoming expedition to Makalu near Mount Everest. This party was comprised of climbers mostly from the San Francisco Bay Area. I had previously heard of Unsoeld as one of Glenn Exum's staff of fine guides in the Teton Range in Wyoming. Although Willi did most of his stateside climbing and guiding in the Tetons, he took part in mountain rescue activities in Washington in the early years.

I later became better acquainted with Willi after he and his wife, Jolene, moved to Seattle and began raising their family of two sons and two daughters.

Prior to Willi's famous Everest summit traverse with Tom Hornbein in 1963, I made a few hikes and climbs with him. We completed an early fall ascent of Mount Washington in Oregon as part of a party that included Jake Breitenbach, who later died on Everest. We also ascended Glacier Peak in Washington with Bob Bates.

Tragically, during a 1976 attempt to climb Nanda Devi in the Himalayas of India, the Unsoeld's daughter, who was named after this peak, collapsed from a stomach ailment and died in Willi's arms at high camp. And three years later, on March 4, 1979, Willi lost his life in an avalanche on Mount Rainier, which also took the life of Janie Diepenbrock, one of his Evergreen College students. It was my sad experience to serve on an investigatory committee that interviewed all the students involved in the winter climb.

A kind and warm personality, Willi Unsoeld was a stimulating educator of youth, forever encouraging them to face life's challenges through the lessons learned in mountaineering.

Dave Mahre

Photo by the author

Among the most active climbers in Washington are those who belong to the small, close-knit group known as the Sherpas, who live in the Ellensburg-Yakima area. Members of this group form the core of Central Washington Mountain Rescue. Among the most active climbers in CWMR were Lex Maxwell, Lynn Buchanan, Bob McCall, and Marcel Schuster of the Yakima area; and Dave Mahre, Gene and Bill Prater, Fred Dunham and Fred Stanley of the Ellensburg Valley.

I met Dave in early September of 1959, when we were involved in a ground-party effort to locate a plane that had crashed into the snow near the summit of Mount Rainier, although I had heard of him earlier. In the 1960s, while teaching for the Olympia Ski School at White Pass, I got better acquainted with Dave, his wife, Mary, and their nine children, who resided in an alpine-style chalet at the base of the chairlift. For several decades, Dave "kept the lifts going" at the ski area. While with the Sherpas, Dave displayed his talents as a writer and skilled sketcher of alpine scenery. He contributed articles and artwork that publicized the climbing exploits of the Sherpas on Mount Rainier and in the Stuart Range.

As one of the pioneering leaders of the Sherpas, Dave made numerous first ascents of peaks in the Stuart Range and pioneered some of the tougher routes on the north flanks of Rainier and Little Tahoma. In 1963, he, Jim Wickwire, Fred Dunham, and Don Anderson made the second ascent of Willis Wall, via a new route up the Central Rib and through the upper ice cap. Dave later completed other new routes on the mountain, via the Russell Cliffs, the North Face of Little Tahoma, and the southern margin of the Mowich Face. While in his fifties, he was finally given the opportunity by Lou Whittaker to participate in two expeditions to Mount Everest. There, on its northern flanks, he did exceptionally well, attaining 26,000 feet in the Great Couloir without the use of supplemental oxygen.

Dave was among those who initiated an annual climb of Mount Adams, to provide a mountain experience for neophyte climbers. Dave Mahre was probably better known to later generations as the father of the Mahre twins, skiers who won the gold and silver medals in the slalom at the 1984 Winter Olympics in Sarajevo.

Bill and Gene Prater

Photo by the author

Bill and Gene Prater were alfalfa farmers in the Kittitas Valley near Ellensburg, within sight of the impressive Mount Stuart massif in the central Cascades. They spent their time off climbing and snowshoeing among the nearby granitic peaks of the Stuart area, and defining new routes up the northeastern slopes of Mount Rainier. They utilized their farm-bred creativity to design their own ice axes and snowshoes, and eventually began marketing their own custom-built "Sherpa" snowshoes, named for the local Sherpas climbing club.

I first heard of Gene in 1957, when he and Marcel Schuster made the first ascent of Curtis Ridge on Mount Rainier, on the same day Pete Schoening and I were making the first ascent of the Wilson Glacier headwall on the opposite side of mountain. The next day, I made a point of meeting the Praters at their farm. I was very impressed by these two ruggedly handsome outdoorsmen and their ingenuity in designing their own snowshoes, ice axes, and other mountaineering gear.

Since then we made several trips together, including a couple of mini-expeditions, with Gene on the 1960 rescue operation on Mount McKinley, and with Bill on the 1965 Mount Kennedy expedition. In 1966, Gene joined me, Jim Wickwire, and Dick Pargeter in the first ascent of Rainier's Central Mowich Face.

Bill studied forestry and mechanical engineering. Gene had a degree in history, and he wrote numerous articles about his climbs, snowshoe design, and techniques, and guidebooks to snowshoe trips in the Cascades. He also led snowshoeing expeditions and taught snowshoeing techniques to members of the Appalachian Mountain Club in New Hampshire's White Mountains. Gene's wife, Yvonne, is also an accomplished historian-author, who wrote several books covering the history of local peaks and passes.

With his wife, Barbara, Bill eventually began producing Sherpa snowshoes full-time by converting a large part of their home in Tacoma into a factory. This worked for a couple of years, but a poor snow year in the 1970s hit the business hard, and they had to sell it to the Tubbs Company in Chicago. They returned to the Ellensburg area, where Bill regained climbing contact with his old Sherpa friends. Gene tragically passed away at age sixty-four after being briefly hospitalized for a growth on his heart.

Photo courtesy of
Lynn Buchanan

Lynn Buchanan

Lynn Buchanan joined the SMRC during the summer of 1952 after participating in a body recovery on Lundin Peak. He maintained his membership there for several years, even after moving to Yakima. In the early 1950s, Lynn helped organize, and also served as president of, Central Washington Mountain Rescue in the Yakima area. Lynn also helped plan and organize, and served as president of, the Washington region of the Mountain Rescue Association. He was often a group leader or lecturer in seminars, teaching mountain search-and-rescue techniques and operations. During his more than fifty-five years and more than three hundred recorded missions while active in mountain rescue, he has been deputized by all five Yakima County Sheriffs because of his personal policy of being ready for any mission.

Lynn was appointed to represent mountain rescue on the state MAST (Military Assistance to Safety and Traffic) Committee, on which he served for many years as a member, and, for seven years, as president. He trained many search-and-rescue units around the state in how to operate around helicopters. He joined the MAST Committee just after the tragic death of an untrained nurse during a helicopter rescue. The committee published a manual and conducted training seminars concerning this issue.

Because Lynn was a fixed-wing pilot, the military pilots looked at him as one who could be trained in more aspects of helicopter operation than those with no flight experience. The result was that he had better training and greater operational experience than many of the other SMRC team members. He was even issued surplus crew equipment to use on missions when necessary. While President of the MAST Committee, he was invited to Olympia to receive, in the Rotunda of the capitol building, a personal commendation from Governor Dan Evans for his efforts in the coordination of civilian and military personnel on search-and-rescue missions in the state of Washington.

Lynn's activism led to his being elected to two terms as president of the Mountain Rescue Association. During that time, some major changes were implemented in the operation of this organization. He was the second president from Washington, following Paul Williams of the SMRC. Since then, there have been two others from Washington, Judy (Beeler) Hanna of Central Washington Mountain Rescue and Fran Sharp of Tacoma Mountain Rescue, the only women to have been elected to that office. In 1976, as president of the MRA, he was invited by a conference of NATO members to speak on special rescue problems in difficult environmental situations at the U.S.A. Bicentennial Emergency Medical Services and Traumatology Conference in Baltimore, Maryland.

In 1978, Lynn participated in a month-long winter Arctic climbing expedition. The team made the first ascent of a previously unclimbed peak and camped on the ice north of the Arctic Circle, miles from any other human habitation.

In his other life, Lynn operated a warehouse and trucking business in Yakima, and served on the Yakima City Council for more than twenty-five years, including one term as mayor. He is still active in mountain-rescue field work. In the fall of 2007, more than a half-century after he began as a rescuer, he participated in a body recovery after a tragic plane crash near Mount Adams.

Lou Whittaker

Photo by the author

I had heard of Jim and Lou Whittaker, the young, athletic mountain-climbing twins of Seattle, about a year before we met at a couple of mountain rescue events. I first met Lou in early October of 1948, during the evacuation of the body of Robert Thorson from high on The Brothers in the Olympic Mountains. Lou started climbing with his twin brother, Jim, at the age of twelve. By the time he was eighteen, he had climbed all the major peaks in Washington. At nineteen, he began guiding on Mount Rainier.

During 1953–54, Lou and Jim served in the Army's Mountain and Cold Weather Training Command at Camp Hale, Colorado, while I was a civilian advisor there. Upon my return from K2 to my job at Camp Hale in late 1953, the Whittakers visited me in my hut and listened to my account of the climb. I think they shared misty eyes with me as I described our tragic loss of Art Gilkey.

Our paths have joined and crossed many times during subsequent mountain search-and-rescue operations, and on Mount Rainier, where Lou has operated the guide service since the early 1960s. He was on his brother Jim's expedition to K2 in 1975 and has since led his own successful expeditions to Kangchenjunga and Mount Everest. His sons, Peter and Win, have served as guides on Rainier, and Peter now leads his own treks and expeditions to various high mountains of the world, including Vinson Massif, the highest peak in Antarctica. Colleen and I have always appreciated the invitations of Lou and his Austrian wife, Ingrid, to attend the mountain guide parties they host at their below-the-ground berm home near Ashford, Washington.

In 1994, Lou collaborated with Andrea Gabbard in the publication of his autobiography, *Lou Whittaker: Memoirs of a Mountain Guide*, which describes mainly his life of travel and mountaineering. In 1969, he co-founded Rainier Mountaineering Inc., the leading guide service on Mount Rainier.

Lou, a legend on Mount Rainier, has made more than 250 summits of the 14,410-foot peak and has led thousands of novice and experienced climbers to the top. He has also climbed in Alaska, the Himalayas, and the Karakoram. In 1984, he led the first successful American climb of the North Col of Mount Everest. The team consisted of guides that had gained much of their knowledge while working for Rainier

Mountaineering Inc. Today, Lou and his wife, Ingrid, spend the winters in Sun Valley, Idaho, and the summers in Ashford. Lou remains an owner and Chief Guide of RMI. While in Ashford, Lou can be seen mingling with climbers at Rainier Base Camp or Whittaker's Bunkhouse. Lou is very involved with many organizations, including the American Lung Association of Washington; he is their honorary chairman for the Climb for Clean Air.

Jim Whittaker

Photo by the author

I met Jim Whittaker in 1949 during a Seattle Mountain Rescue Council gathering at Snoqualmie Pass. Jim and Lou began guiding at Paradise in 1951, while I was a park ranger there, so we socialized quite a bit in those days. We also worked together briefly at Camp Hale.

In 1963, Jim achieved the distinction of being the first American to summit Mount Everest, which has provided him with countless opportunities to enrich his life in many ways. In 1965, I was with him when he led Senator Robert F. Kennedy on the first ascent of Mount Kennedy in Canada's Yukon Territory.

For many years, Jim served as manager of REI in Seattle, helping to build it into a multimillion dollar operation, with many branch stores throughout the United States.

To provide them with a memorable experience, Jim led a large party of disabled outdoors enthusiasts up Mount Rainier. Both he and Lou have donated the proceeds of some of their climbs to fund-raising efforts, including the fights against cancer and heart disease.

After Jim led Senator Robert Kennedy up Mount Kennedy, a peak in the Canadian Yukon named for his slain brother, he became close friends with Bobby and the Kennedy family, joining them often at Hyannis Port, Hickory Hill (RFK's home in Virginia) and on skiing, river rafting, sailing and other adventures. Jim invited me to share with him a weekend visit with Ethel Kennedy and family at the Hickory Hill estate in McLean, Virginia—a most memorable experience. He was the Washington state campaign chairman for Senator Kennedy in 1968. He was at the Senator's bedside when he died, and served as one of his pallbearers at Arlington National Cemetery.

In 1978, Jim Whittaker, after five American failures spanning forty years, organized and led the first successful American ascent of K2, the world's second highest, and many say most dangerous, peak. Also, against formidable political and logistical odds, he organized and led the spectacularly successful 1990 Mount Everest Peace Climb, which put twenty men and women from three superpowers—the United States, China, and the Soviet Union—on the summit of Everest. This ascent was designed to help focus world attention on environmental issues. In the process, the team removed two tons of garbage left on the mountain by previous expeditions.

With his wife, photographer Dianne Roberts, Whittaker designed and built a stunning log home, dubbed by their friends the "Taj Macabin," overlooking the Strait of Juan de Fuca in Port Townsend, Washington. An accomplished blue water sailor, he twice skippered his own boat on the 2,400-mile Victoria, Canada to Maui, Hawaii sailing race. Whittaker also sailed his ketch, named Impossible, with his wife and two teenage sons, Joss and Leif, from Port Townsend, Washington to Mexico, the Marquesas Islands, the Tuamotus, the Society Islands (Tahiti, Moorea, and Bora Bora), the Cook Islands, American Samoa, Fiji, Vanuatu, New Caledonia, Australia and then back to the United States, a journey of more than twenty thousand miles.

In September 1999, Jim's autobiography, *A Life on the Edge: Memoirs of Everest and Beyond,* was published by The Mountaineers Books in Seattle, Washington. He traveled throughout the United States on a book promotion tour, appeared on countless television programs and in other media, and autographed thousands of copies of his book. It was awarded the year 2000 Pacific Northwest Bookseller's Association Award for Literary Excellence in the memoir category. A paperback version was released in September 2000.

Glenn Kelsey

A small, wiry man of great strength, Glenn Kelsey of Bremerton was among the early leaders of Olympic Mountain Rescue. Glenn participated in a great number of operations throughout the Olympics. Somewhat surprisingly, much of the early rescue activity took place in Kitsap County. At that time, there were no local lowland rescue groups, and OMR was regularly called to serve in that capacity. The group searched for lost hunters and fishermen, sought runaways, found downed aircraft, and once even saved a little old lady sitting on a stump near her back yard.

Glenn Kelsey was among the OMR members who went to Mount McKinley in 1960 to support the John Day party rescue effort. This was probably the most noteworthy mission in which OMR ever participated. For Glenn, it was quite a shock being transported directly from sea level and the Seattle rain to the high altitude and sub-zero temperature of Mount McKinley.

Sadly, Glenn was among the shipyard workers who contracted cancer via the inhalation of asbestos dust. He passed away prematurely, which was a great loss to those who knew him in the mountaineering community of Bremerton.

Bob McCall

A veteran of the Army's 10th Mountain Division during World War II, and among the early chairmen of the CWMR, Bob McCall was an instructor at Yakima Valley College. He also taught in the White Pass Ski School for many winters. In 1955, Bob made the second ski descent of Mount Rainier, via the Emmons Glacier. He also took part in a first ascent of the northeast wall of Little Tahoma. Among the highlights of his work in mountain rescue was a helicopter evacuation from the north wall of Mount Stuart, an operation that could not have been successful without his technical skill and courage.

John Simac and Lee Tegner at Camp Schurman   Photo courtesy of John Simac

John Simac, Lee Tegner and **Bert Brown** were among the early leaders of Tacoma Mountain Rescue and served many years in important capacities in that group. In particular, Simac and Tegner were deeply involved for several summers in the transport of supplies for and actual construction of the Schurman Cabin at Steamboat Prow on Mount Rainier. Simac also constructed the climbing wall that has been an important "backyard" feature of the climbing classes at the clubroom of the Tacoma chapter of The Mountaineers.

Judy Beehler Hanna

Photo courtesy of
Judy Hanna

Although Judy Hanna entered the mountain rescue scene after 1965, she deserves a mention here, because in 1980 she became the first female president of the Mountain Rescue Association, and served in that capacity for two years. Upon leaving that position, she became the executive secretary of the MRA, and she remained so until 1992.

I first met Judy at a mountaineering function in Yakima, Washington. In 1966, Judy participated in the first of several annual "mass climbs" of Mount Adams. There she became acquainted with members of Central Washington Mountain Rescue. Within two years, she became a member of the unit. She was a school teacher, and most of her free time was devoted to her rescue unit and to climbing.

During the 1970s, Judy attended almost all of the MRA meetings. She and another member of CWMR were added to the Seattle Mountain Rescue Council roster for a time, allowing them to fly weekend standbys with the military MAST (Military Assistance to Safety and Traffic) unit at Gray Army Airfield. She attained experience administering medicine in the field, and she spent evenings helping in the emergency room at a Yakima hospital.

APPENDIX B ∿

Selected Mountain Rescue Leadership in Oregon

Over the years, I met many of the leading figures involved in search and rescue on Mount Hood when I was at Timberline Lodge to either register for a climb or attend the outdoor-oriented programs presented there. The Lodge and its alpine environs have been the locale for gatherings of such groups as the Mazamas, The Mountaineers of Seattle, The American Alpine Club, the Seattle Mountain Rescue Council and its affiliates, the Wilderness Society, and the 10th Mountain Division Association.

On several occasions I met with lodge manager Dick Kohnstamm while I was preparing a painting of the Timberline Ski Area. And, of course, I've always envied the lodge's huge St. Bernards, with their lazy lives of enhancing the local Alpine atmosphere.

I apologize in advance to rescuers that were not mentioned or received less coverage than they deserve in this volume. It is hoped that this book will motivate others to write more about the people who had an important role in mountain rescue.

Photo courtesy of
Anne Harlow Trussell
and the Mazamas

Ole Lien

Ole Lien, a premier solo mountaineer, retired after an astounding four hundred and forty-four ascents of Mount Hood. Born in 1898, he remained a member of the Mazamas until 1960, and he was on good terms with members of the Wy'east Climbers. He continued working on and off for the U.S. Forest Service until 1960, supplementing his income with odd jobs in Government Camp. Even in retirement, he was unable to avoid adventure. In 1964, while living in his sister's vacation cabin by the Sandy River, he was forced to evacuate the structure before it was swept away in a massive flood. As he grew older, Lien became increasingly reclusive. In the spring of 1972 he suffered a stroke, and he passed away in January of 1973.

Photo courtesy of
Wy'east Climbers

Ray Atkeson

Ray Atkeson was a famous photographer of Northwest mountain scenes and a charter member of the Wy'east Climbers. He also enjoyed a decades-long association with the Mazamas. The publication of a series of books featuring his photos of Oregon made him one of the most recognizable photographers in the Pacific Northwest. In 1987, he was made an honorary member of the Mazamas, an honor bestowed on only a handful of people in the club's century of existence. Atkeson received many more honors during his later years: the Governor's Award for the Arts, the Distinguished Citizen of Oregon Award, and an honorary Doctor of Fine Arts degree from Linfield College. In 1988, Oregon Governor Neil Goldschmidt bestowed upon Atkeson the title of Oregon's Photographer Laureate in recognition of his sixty-two years of pioneering work in the field of photography.

Atkeson was also a friend to other non-profit organizations. He donated his time and talents to institutions such as the Audubon Society, the Sierra Club, the Oregon Natural Resources Council, the Nature Conservancy and the Friends of the Columbia Gorge. He also served as a spokesman for the effort to expand and improve the quality of Oregon's Scenic Waterways System.

I first met Ray in the fall of 1952 while I was a park ranger at Mount Rainier, when he came up to photograph some fall color around Reflection Lake. In later years, I met his equally talented photographer wife, Mira, at their hilltop home in southwest Portland. I was honored by Ray's request that I draw landform maps for a couple of his photo-essay coffee-table books on the mountains of the Pacific Northwest.

During the last decade of his life, Atkeson's eyesight began to dim, but with the assistance of his son, he was able to complete *Wind on the Waves,* a beautiful look at the Oregon coast that was co-authored by Rick Schafer and Kim Stafford. In late 1989, at the age of eighty-three, Atkeson was diagnosed with colon cancer. Refusing to undergo chemotherapy or related treatment, Ray opted to live out the remaining months of his life in peace with his family, friends and the comforts of his own home.

Everett Darr

Photo courtesy of
Anne Harlow Trussell
and the Mazamas

Born in 1907, Everett Darr remained a member of The
American Alpine Club, Mazamas and Wy'east Climbers
until his death in 1981. He led successful ascents for all
three organizations, but is best remembered for his
business ventures. The climbing packs he created are
considered collector's items, as are his Wy'east brand ice
axes and crampons. The ice axes and crampons were sold only for two
years before the war and one or two after the war until his supplies ran
out. They are quite rare today. For nearly twenty years, he rented skis
and equipment out of a small building in Government Camp, where he
was well known to younger climbers and skiers. In his later years, Darr
and his wife, Ida, enjoyed collecting and polishing agates.

My only clear recollection of meeting Everett and his wife was during
a fog-bound evening at their Rock Shop in Government Camp. There
he gave my young sons a few beautiful pieces of rock, along with advice
on where to lay out our sleeping bags for the night. Everett made forty-
nine ascents of Mount Hood, and extended his climbing to other areas,
including leading a group up spectacular St. Peters Dome in the
Columbia Gorge.

Randall Kester

Photo courtesy of
John McCormick

Randall Kester has been a Portland lawyer for more than
sixty-three years. He served as president of the Mazamas
from 1950–1951. In addition to being President of The
Mount Hood Ski Patrol, he was a member of the
National Ski Patrol. He was one of the founders and first
president of the Mountain Rescue and Safety Council of Oregon, a
predecessor of the present Portland Mountain Rescue. He ceased his
mountaineering pursuits in 1957, when he was appointed as a Justice of
the Oregon Supreme Court. After his days on the bench, he became the
General Solicitor for the Union Pacific Railroad in the Pacific
Northwest. He was quite active with the Boy Scouts and continues to
practice law for the Cosgrave Vergeer Kester firm.

Photo courtesy of
Wy'east Climbers

Joe Leuthold

Born in 1906, Joe Leuthold, arguably the most respected member of the Wy'east Climbers, would not live long enough to enjoy retirement. After serving with the 10th Mountain Division during World War II, he was hired by Everett Darr to run the Summit Ski area. He was also a member of the Mazamas, the Mountain Rescue and Safety Council of Oregon, and the Mount Hood Ski Patrol. He served in several key positions that helped shape the direction of these respected organizations. In 1964, the Mazamas created a plaque bearing his name, which recognized him as a climber who led club-sponsored ascents of the sixteen major northwest peaks. This plaque is still awarded each year at the Mazamas annual banquet to those few who qualify. Leuthold made sixty-four ascents of Mount Hood and led some of the most historic first ascents in the Cascades and Columbia River Gorge. To the shock and disbelief of many friends and colleagues, Joe died of cancer on December 12, 1965.

A few years after his passing, more than forty of his friends and family members attended a high-altitude ceremony in his honor. On a needle of rock on Mount Hood's Illumination Saddle, this group of admirers placed a brass plaque listing the organizations Joe belonged to and enjoyed serving. In 1970, the Oregon Geographic Names Board officially named the chute above Mount Hood's Reid Glacier "Leuthold Couloir." This climbing route is a fitting tribute to a man whose name still stands for strength, talent, and kindness.

Photo courtesy of
Rick Lorenz

Hank Lewis

With a clear memory at the age of ninety-six in 2008, Hank Lewis still enjoys the alpine environment that he was first introduced to in the summer of 1921. During World War II, Hank served in the Army's 10th Mountain Division.

Hank served as the first rescue chairman for the Mountain Rescue and Safety Council of Oregon. He also was a key member during the 1930s through the 1960s, the "Golden Age" of the Wy'east Climbers. Hank served during 1954–55 as president of the MRA.

Lewis was employed by the Chase Bag Company for many years and enjoyed climbing wherever his job happened to take him. He took extensive cross-country ski trips, including circling the rim of Crater Lake and making orbital trips around Mount St. Helens and Mount Hood. In the early 1970s, he trekked to the base camp of Mount Everest with fellow Wy'easter Al Combs. Hank never kept track of how many times he climbed Mount Hood, but most remarkable of all is the sheer length of his career on the mountain. His first ascent took place in 1921, and his last in 1986, sixty-five years later.

In 1937, the U.S. Forest Service hired Lewis for $10 a weekend to render services and organize a formal ski patrol at Timberline Lodge. Lewis provided his own equipment, using an old, roll-nosed toboggan from the Wy'east cabin, and learned first aid in a class in Portland. Working with members of the club and other interested individuals, he provided assistance to injured skiers. The Mount Hood Ski Patrol was formally organized and incorporated March 2, 1938, with fifty members and Hank Lewis as patrol chief.

In May 2008, I met with Hank Lewis in Gig Harbor, Washington, during the annual get-together of the Mount Rainier and Northwest chapters of the 10th Mountain Division Association. Hank talked of his experiences as a skier, climber, and mountain rescuer in the Mount Hood area. He was still able to recall many of his missions, but both of us are so hearing-impaired that we almost butted heads during our chat.

Russ McJury

Russ McJury was born in 1916 and served in the 10th Mountain Division during World War II. After the end of the war, he joined Raffi Bedayn and my brother K in an ascent of Mont Blanc via its southwest ridge, which rises above Courmayeur.

Upon his return home in 1945, Russ continued to make history on Mount Hood. In 1951, accompanied by David Young and fellow Wy'easter Dave Wagstaff, he made the first complete ascent of Castle Crags. Also known as Hawkin's Cliff, this route is up a notoriously crumbling rock buttress, sometimes considered more technically challenging than Yocum Ridge if conditions are at their worst. McJury also made numerous ascents in the North Cascades. He served as President of the Wy'east Climbers in 1952.

McJury's last ascent of Mount Hood occurred in 1983, when he was sixty-seven years old. That year marked his fiftieth anniversary ascent of Mount Hood and, accompanied by close personal friends, he made his way up the West Crater Rim Route on the southern side of the mountain. It was a fitting end to a remarkable climbing career.

Harold Engles

Harold Engles led a legendary life in the U.S. Forest Service, serving for many years in Mount Hood National Forest and operating out of the Timberline Lodge area. He then moved to the North Cascades of Washington, where he served many more years in trail design and maintenance, and as District Ranger in the Mount Baker National Forest. It was my pleasure to finally meet him and his wife at his farm home near Darrington, only a short time before he passed on. But he was still a tall, suntanned man with a sparkle in his eye, and he had many memories of his Forest Service days in the hills.

Ralph Wiese

During World War II, Ralph Wiese served briefly with the 87th Mountain Infantry Regiment at Fort Lewis. On Mount Rainier, he tested equipment and techniques for eventual use in combat. After that, he served with the

Photo courtesy of
John McCormick

North American Wing of the Air Transport Command in Labrador as a dog-team driver searching for downed aircraft. At that time, some pilots ferrying bombers from Labrador to England became confused by the magnetic pole while navigating and either got lost or crashed. Later, he manned a high-arctic weather station for the U.S. Air Force.

After graduating with a forestry degree from Oregon State College and joining the U.S. Forest Service, Wiese was assigned to conduct avalanche research at Mount Baker in Washington. There was a big push by the Forest Service to get avalanche information, in case it was needed for the 1960 Winter Olympics at Squaw Valley, California.

In 1953, Wiese was transferred to the Glacier District of the Mount Hood National Forest at Government Camp. His duties included being a liaison with Timberline Lodge, Mount Hood Ski Patrol and local businesses, and conducting area search and rescue. He finished his Forest

Service career in Medford in the Rogue River National Forest, where he was involved in the development of the Mount Ashland Ski Area.

I met Ralph Wiese in the summer of 1950, while doing some geological reconnaissance in the North Cascades with my University of Washington Professor Peter Misch. At that time, Ralph was the District Ranger working out of the office in Glacier, Washington. He joined Pete and I in a presumed first ascent of what we named "Forgotten Peak," which rises high above the Nooksack River Valley. However, upon our arrival at the summit after a 3,000-foot brush-fighting climb, we found the proverbial sardine can there, and later learned that, according to "Beckey's Bible" (*A Climber's Guide to the Cascade and Olympic Mountains of Washington* written by Fred Beckey), we had climbed Mount Sefrit. Ralph passed away in 1985.

Bill Hackett

Bill Hackett was perhaps the most ambitious climber to emerge from the golden age of climbing on Mount Hood. As a veteran of the 10th Mountain Division during World War II, he became a career Army officer and used his position to train troops for cold-weather combat. He reached the summit of Mount Hood eighty-eight times and summited McKinley four times during five expeditions. With successful ascents of McKinley, Cerro Aconcagua, Kilimanjaro, Mont Blanc, Mount Kosciusko, and an attempt on Vinson Massif, Hackett helped establish the Seven Summits dream—the attainment of the highest peak on each of the seven continents. He additionally organized and led the 1960 German-American Karakoram Expedition to K2. Though forced to retreat as a result of serious storms, his attempt is considered by many to be the last of the "colonial" expeditions to the toughest mountain in the world. He was made an honorary member of the Mazamas in 1989 and passed away suddenly in a hospital on August 9, 1999, due to complications following a heart operation. The story of Bill's life and world travels was published in the 2002 book *Climb to Glory: The Adventures of Bill Hackett*, by Ric Conrad and June Hackett.

Dick Pooley

Dick Pooley, first Mountain Rescue Association president, wearing his Hood River Crag Rats outfit in 1954.

At the age of eighty-eight, Dick Pooley is still active in the MRA in Oregon. His first climb of Mount Hood was the annual American Legion climb up the peak's south side in 1938. In 1939, he studied radio technology at Manual Arts Evening High School and National School in Los Angeles. Upon earning his ham radio license, he enlisted in the military and served mostly in the South Pacific. On the GI Bill, Dick earned his degree from Oregon State College in 1949, and then entered the radio-communications business. He was Chief Engineer for KBKW in Portland, and then went to work for Tektronix in 1958.

In 1946, Dick moved to Hood River, became a member of the Crag Rats and climbed all of the local volcanoes. He then went back to Portland, where he joined the Mazamas in 1953. He became a leader of many club climbs and started a program to reduce the size of the club's climbing parties. In 1963, he was elected to a three-year term on the Mazamas executive council. He became their vice president in 1964.

Pooley joined the Wy'east Climbers in 1956, The American Alpine Club in 1961, and served on the Mount Hood Ski Patrol starting in 1963. Of all his service on Mount Hood, he is probably best known for his extensive work in the latter organization. In 1955, he became a member of the Mountain Rescue and Safety Council of Oregon, and served as its president in 1958, 1959, 1968, and 1969. He was a charter member and first president of the Mountain Rescue Association. Dick was active in teaching climbing and mountain rescue techniques on the Eliot Glacier. Ham radio remained a driving interest throughout his life and, through this, he met and married Carolyn Nelson, another ham operator.

Ross Petrie

Ross Petrie was born on July 25th, 1926, in Auckland, New Zealand. His father came from the Shetland Islands and his mother came from London, England. The family arrived in the Pacific Northwest in the early 1930s. His father immediately started his family on a lifetime of car camping. All six of them piled into a Model-A Ford loaded down with camping gear and plied the Oregon Coast on many of their early outdoor experiences. At that time, the Oregon Coast was mostly a wilderness area.

During his grade- and high-school years, Ross spent a great deal of time learning water safety skills and swim racing at the YMCA in Portland. His activities at the YMCA led to five summers at Camp Meehan at the base of Mount St. Helens. There he learned the fundamentals of multiple-day backpacking, mountain climbing, and leadership. His first ascent of Mount St. Helens was at age thirteen.

During the early forties, Ross took up skiing at Mount Hood. He hitchhiked back and forth to the mountain and learned the sport on his own. There were no ski lifts, so he gained the top of the hill by climbing it on skis. He often made two runs a day between Timberline Lodge and Government Camp, with three miles and two thousand feet of altitude gain each trip. Later, he had little money to spend on skiing, so he joined the Mount Hood Ski Patrol. This provided him with a lift ticket and a place to sleep. In sixty-five years of active skiing as a ski patrolman, ski instructor and Forest Service snow ranger, he never paid for a lift ticket at Mount Hood. Ski patrolling soon blossomed into mountain rescue, and over the years, he took part in many searches and rescues.

One of the high points of Petrie's mountain rescue career was being rushed, on a moment's notice, to Mount McKinley to take part in the John Day rescue. It turned out that he didn't get above the base camp level, but he still considered it a grand experience. A second noteworthy experience occurred during an evacuation on the North Sister. While moving the victim, Ross fell about seventy-five feet off the steep snow slope just below the summit. Fortunately, he was uninjured, so he brushed himself off, and climbed back up to finish his day's work.

In the mid 1940s, Ross and his friend, Dave Pearson, were the first to go to Smith Rocks specifically to climb. It is now a popular climbing area.

Ross's British mother, with her Victorian sensibilities, never really understood the hazards of what he was doing, so she never worried about his experiences in the mountains. His father, on the other hand, who came from the Isle of Unst in the North Sea, thought that such adventures were good for growing boys.

Photo courtesy of
the Petrie family

Keith Petrie

Keith Petrie, Ross Petrie's younger brother, began his mountaineering career in 1939 with his first climb, at age eleven, of Mount St. Helens, while attending the Portland YMCA Camp Meehan on Spirit Lake. He climbed Mount St. Helens sixteen times during the next five years. He started skiing while in grade school. He joined the Mount Hood Ski Patrol in 1944, where he was involved in several rescues. He also served as patrol chief for three years and president for one year. While attending Oregon State College, Keith led weekend mountaineering activities for their mountain club. Keith graduated from the School of Forestry at Oregon State College in 1952. He then served as a professional forester for fifteen years, working in private industry in timber management, timber cruising, reforestation projects, and fire control.

In 1955, he became a founding member of the Mountain Rescue and Safety Council of Oregon, eventually serving as rescue director from 1956–61. Keith introduced the akia rescue sled (imported from Austria) in 1958 for both mountain rescue and ski patrol use. Keith participated in numerous rescue missions on the major volcanoes of Oregon and the walls and spires of the Columbia Gorge, along with the 1960 Mount McKinley rescue of the John Day party. Among his most difficult missions was a body recovery from the east face of Mount Thielson, Oregon, which involved a 560-foot vertical lift by a cable system.

He was then employed in the ski industry, first for Mount Hood Meadows during its development and construction, and then as general manager during its early years of operation. Subsequently, he managed the ski areas at Anthony Lakes in northeastern Oregon, Mount Spokane in Washington, and the Multorpor Ski Bowl complex at Government Camp, Oregon. Keith served eleven years as President of the Pacific Northwest Ski Areas Association, and six years on the board of directors of the National Ski Areas Association, serving on both the marketing and the community development committees. In 1984, Keith assumed the position of executive director of the Mount Hood Recreation Association, the Oregon Ski Areas Association, and the Oregon Ski Industries Association. Keith represented the ski industry in the Oregon State Legislature for twenty-five years, until his retirement in 1993.

Keith also served as a member and Chairman of the Oregon Winter Recreation Advisory Council, which advises the Department of

Transportation on the development of Oregon's Snow Park program. In 1978, he was appointed by the Governor of Oregon to the Advisory Committee to the State Department of Tourism. In 1994, Keith received, from the Portland Oregon Visitor's Association, The Portlandia Award, which "recognizes the greatest overall contribution to the promotion of tourism in Portland and Oregon."

Ray Conkling

Photo courtesy of
Ray Conkling

Ray Conkling has been active in Portland Mountain Rescue since the 1960s. He graduated from Oregon State University with a bachelor's degree in Forestry. However, his professional life was as a photographer and owner of Conkling Inc., a photography and photo-processing shop in Portland. Besides mountain rescue volunteerism, including participation in the rescue of the John Day party on Mount McKinley in 1960, Ray has climbed widely, summiting most of the major peaks in the Northwest, and climbing frequently in the Tetons and Colorado, in addition to summiting Mount Fuji and peaks in the Northern Alps of Japan.

Constitution of the Mountain Rescue Association, Adopted June 7, 1959

MISSION STATEMENT

A volunteer public service organization dedicated to the saving of lives through rescue and public safety education.

PURPOSE

The purpose of this organization shall be to provide a central agency through which the efforts and activities of member units may be coordinated to more effectively promote mountain safety education, and to provide integrated mountain rescue service, to promote the free exchange of rescue techniques and procedures, to disseminate advances in equipment and to promote standardization thereof as much as is possible.

BY-LAWS

ARTICLE I **Name**

SECTION I. The name of this organization shall be the Mountain Rescue Association.

ARTICLE II **Headquarters**

SECTION I. The association headquarters shall be located at the address of the Executive Secretary unless some other address is designated by the Board of Directors.

ARTICLE III **Membership**

SECTION I. The individual mountain rescue units shall in themselves be members of the Association.

SECTION II. Membership shall be open to any rescue unit or organization approved by the Board of Directors.

SECTION III.   The Board of Directors shall establish recommended minimum membership requirements for membership in the individual mountain rescue units and organizations and shall establish uniform emblems.

SECTION IV.   Governmental rescue units shall be recognized as ex officio members. They shall not be subject to assessment.

ARTICLE IV   Board of Directors

SECTION I.   There shall be a Board of Directors consisting of one delegate from each of the member units or organizations. Each delegate shall have one vote. There shall be in addition an alternate delegate from each unit or organization who may vote in the absence of the delegate. The alternate delegate must be from the same unit or organization.

SECTION II.   The entire management and government of the Association, except as otherwise expressly provided herein, shall be invested in the Board of Directors.

SECTION III.   Delegates and alternate delegates to the Board of Directors shall be designated by their units for terms of one year. Foresaid delegates shall be designated prior to the annual meeting, which shall be held in conjunction with a spring conference, and shall hold office until the spring conference of the following year.

ARTICLE V   Officers

SECTION I.   The Board of Directors shall elect annually, to serve from spring conference to spring conference, a President, Vice President, Secretary, Treasurer and Executive Secretary, and such other officers as the Board deems necessary. The President and Vice President shall be elected within the Board and shall be the President and Vice President of the Mountain Rescue Association.

SECTION II.   President, Vice President, Secretary and Treasurer and Executive Secretary shall serve no more than two consecutive terms.

ARTICLE VI   Duties of Officers

SECTION I.   The President shall perform the duties usually devolving upon his office. He shall appoint, subject to confirmation by the Board of Directors, all committee chairmen, and subject to like confirmation, shall fill all vacancies in committee chairmen.

SECTION II.   The Vice President shall act in place of the President in his absence and during the President's absence shall have all his powers and duties.

SECTION III.   The Secretary and Treasurer shall perform the usual duties devolving upon their office, except as otherwise provided by the Board. They shall provide reports on Association activities as the Board requires.

SECTION IV.   The duties of the Executive Secretary shall be designated by the Board of Directors.

ARTICLE VII   Committees

SECTION I.   The Board of Directors may delegate the management of any of the properties of the Association and the performance of its several activities to such committees or committee as it sees fit.

SECTION II.   All committee chairmen shall be appointed by the President subject to confirmation by the Board of Directors, and all committee chairmen vacancies shall be filled by the President, subject to like confirmation.

ARTICLE VIII   Publications

SECTION I.   The Association shall regularly publish a newsletter to all members of the Association to disseminate information on equipment, rescue techniques and information of general interest.

ARTICLE IX   Meetings

SECTION I.   The Board meetings shall be held at such times and places and upon such notice as the Board may direct. Meetings shall be held at least semi-annually, one meeting in conjunction with an annual conference during the month of June for demonstration and instruction in the field of rescue techniques. The Board may delegate to an officer the authority to call meetings and to give notice thereof.

SECTION II.   A quorum shall consist of 51 percent of the total membership.

ARTICLE X   **Dues**

SECTION I.   Dues shall be those as are set by the Board of Directors.

ARTICLE XI   **Rules of Order**

SECTION I.   Roberts Rules of Order, revised, shall govern in all parliamentary matters.

ARTICLE XII   **Amendments**

SECTION I.   By-laws of this organization may be amended by a two thirds majority vote at a duly called meeting of the Board of Directors.

SECTION II.   Provided, however, the sponsor of an amendment to the By-laws must give written notice to all members of the association of the proposed amendment at least sixty (60) days prior to the meeting. Provided further that the membership rolls shall be available to all members of the Association.

SECTION III.   In the event that delegate or alternate delegate does not attend the meeting at which a vote is taken upon a proposed amendment to the By-laws, the member organization may vote upon the proposed amendment by registered mail directed to the President, provided that foresaid letter must be received prior to the meeting.

Dated this 7th day of June, 1959,
at Timberline Lodge,
Mount Hood, Oregon

Presidents of the Mountain Rescue Association, 1959–2009

1. **Richard R. "Dick" Pooley**, Hood River Crag Rats, Oregon, 1959–1961
2. **Dorrell E. Looff**, Seattle Mountain Rescue, Washington, 1961–1963
3. **John W. Arens**, Hood River Crag Rats, Oregon, 1963–1965
4. **Vance R. Yost**, Altadena Mountain Rescue, California, 1965–1967
5. **Kenneth C. Carpenter**, Everett Mountain Rescue, Washington, 1967–1969
6. **Ray Neal**, Southern Arizona Rescue Association, Arizona, 1969–1970
7. **Dave Moore**, Alpine Rescue Team, Colorado, 1970–1972
8. **Paul M. Williams**, Seattle Mountain Rescue, Washington, 1972–1974
9. **Lynn Buchanan**, Central Washington Mountain Rescue, Washington, 1974–1975
10. **Phil Umholtz**, Bay Area Mountain Rescue Unit, California, 1975–1978
11. **Chuck Demarest**, Rocky Mountain Rescue Group, Colorado, 1978–1980
12. **Judy Hanna**, Central Washington Mountain Rescue, Washington, 1980–1982
13. **Arnold Gaffrey**, Sierra Madre Search and Rescue, California, 1982–1984
14. **Abbe J. Keith**, Sierra Madre Search and Rescue, California, 1984–1986
15. **Walt Walker**, Riverside Mountain Rescue Unit, California, 1986–1988
16. **Hunter Holloway**, Alpine Rescue Team, Colorado, 1988–1990
17. **Drew Davis**, Larimer County Search and Rescue, Colorado, 1990–1991
18. **Dick Bethers**, Salt Lake County Search and Rescue, Utah, 1991–1993
19. **Kevin Walker**, Riverside Mountain Rescue Unit, California 1993–1995
20. **Tim Cochrane**, Vail Mountain Rescue Group, Colorado, 1995–1998
21. **Tim Kovacs**, Central Arizona Mountain Rescue Association, Arizona, 1998–2000
22. **Rocky Henderson**, Portland Mountain Rescue, Oregon 2000–2002
23. **Dan Hourihan**, Alaska Mountain Rescue Group, Alaska, 2002–2004
24. **Monty Bell**, San Diego Mountain Rescue, California, 2004–2006
25. **Fran Sharp**, Tacoma Mountain Rescue, Washington, 2006–2008
26. **Charley Shimanski**, Alpine Rescue Team, Colorado, 2008–

Selected Bibliography

American Alpine Club, The, 1951–1955, 1961, 2007. *Accidents in North American Mountaineering* (annual editions): The American Alpine Club, New York and Golden, Colorado.

Annala, Eino, 1976. *The Crag Rats*: Hood River News, Hood River, Oregon.

Beckey, Fred, 1949. *A Climber's Guide to the Cascade and Olympic Mountains of Washington.* Frequently updated editions titled *Cascade Alpine Guide* (3 volumes): The Mountaineers Books, Seattle.

Blanchard, Smoke, 1985. *Walking Up and Down in the World: Memories of a Mountain Rambler*: Sierra Club Books, San Francisco.

Conrad, Ric, 2003. *Mount Hood: Adventures of the Wy'east Climbers.* Unpublished manuscript.

Conrad, Ric, and June Hackett, 2002. *Climb to Glory: The Adventures of Bill Hackett*: K2 Books, Beaverton, Oregon.

Coombs, H. A., 1936. *The Geology of Mount Rainier National Park* (Vol. 3, No. 2): University of Washington Press, Seattle.

Crandell, Dwight R., and Donal R. Mullineaux, 1967. "Volcanic Hazards at Mount Rainier, Washington." U.S. Geological Survey Bulletin 1238.

Farabee, Charles R. "Butch", 1998. *Death, Daring and Disaster: Search and Rescue in the National Parks*: Roberts Rinehart, Boulder, Colorado.

Fisk, Richard S., Clifford A. Hopson, and Aaron C. Waters, 1963. "Geology of Mount Rainier National Park, Washington." U.S. Geological Survey Professional Paper 444.

Grauer, Jack, 1996. *Mount Hood: A Complete History* (multiple editions): Self-published.

Harris, Stephen L., 1988, *Fire Mountains of the West: The Cascade and Mono Lake Volcanoes.* Mountain Press, Missoula, Montana.

Hopson, C. A., A. G. Waters, V. R. Bender, and Meyer Rubin, 1962. "The Latest Eruption from Mount Rainier Volcano." *Journal of Geology* (Vol. 70, No. 6), pp 635–647.

Houston, Charles S., 1980. *Going High: The Story of Man and Altitude*: The American Alpine Club, Golden, Colorado.

Mariner, Wastl, 1948. *Mountain Rescue Techniques:* Frohnweiler, Innsbruck, Austria. English translation by Kurt Beam and Dr. Otto Trott, 1963, distributed by The Mountaineers Books, Seattle.

Meyer, Richard D., 1996, *Mountain Rescues with Ome Daiber*. Self-published.

Milne, Malcom, 1968. *The Book of Modern Mountaineering*: G. P. Putnam's Sons: New York.

Molenaar, Dee, 1971. *The Challenge of Rainier: A Record of the Explorations and Ascents, Triumphs and Tragedies on the Northwest's Greatest Mountain*: The Mountaineers Books, Seattle.

Molenaar, Dee, 2008. *High and Wide with Sketchpad: Memoirs and Images of a Dinosaur Mountaineer*. Unpublished manuscript.

Mountaineers, The, 1960, *Mountaineering: The Freedom of the Hills* (multiple updated editions): The Mountaineers Books, Seattle.

Mullineaux, Donal R., Robert S. Sigafoos, and E. L. Hendricks, 1969. "A Historic Eruption and Mount Rainier, Washington". U.S. Geological Survey Professional Paper 650-D, pp. D15–D18.

Olsen, Jack, 1998. *The Climb Up to Hell:* Griffin, New York.

Olympic Mountain Rescue, 2006. *Olympic Mountains: A Climbing Guide*. The Mountaineers Books, Seattle.

Orlob, Helen, 1963. *Mountain Rescues:* Thomas Nelson & Sons, New York.

Rusk, Charles E., 1924, *Tales of a Western Mountaineer*. Houghton Mifflin, Boston. (1978 reprint by The Mountaineers Books, Seattle).

Russell, I.C., 1898, "Glaciers at Mount Rainier." U.S. Geological Survey 18th Annual Report, 1896–97, part 2, pp. 349–415.

Sholes, Charles H., 1923. *Mazama: A Record of Mountaineering in the Pacific Northwest:* J. H. Williams, Tacoma, Washington.

Simpson, Joe, 1993. *This Game of Ghosts:* The Mountaineers Books, Seattle.

Smith, Esther K., 2006. "Crag Rats at 80." *Hood River News*, Aug. 23, 2006.

Smoot, Jeff, 1992. *Summit Guide to the Cascade Volcanoes:* Chockstone Press, Evergreen, Colorado.

Van Tilburg, Christopher, M.D., 2007. *Mountain Rescue Doctor: Wilderness Medicine in the Extremes of Nature:* St. Martin's Press, New York.

Whittaker, Jim, 1999. *A Life on the Edge: Memoirs of Everest and Beyond:* The Mountaineers Books, Seattle.

Whittaker, Lou, and Andrea Gabbard, 1994. *Lou Whittaker: Memoirs of a Mountain Guide:* The Mountaineers Books, Seattle.

Williams, J. H., 1912. *The Guardians of the Columbia: Mount Hood, Mount Adams, and Mount St. Helens*. Self-published.

Williams, Paul, 1987. *Oregon Coast Hikes:* The Mountaineers Books, Seattle.

Of the aforementioned authors, Jack Grauer and Ric Conrad deserve special mention and appreciation for allowing me to utilize material from their publications and manuscripts.

Jack Grauer earned a degree in journalism at Oregon State University, and, during World War II, he served as a radio technician in the Army Air Force in the southwestern Pacific. A member of the Mazamas since 1947, Jack served in several leadership roles in the club, including president and director of their climbing school and field trips. Jack has traveled widely throughout the ranges of the western United States and Canada, Alaska, and Hawaii. He saw the world with a knapsack, and rode the railroad through Siberia, from Vladivostok on the Asian coast back to Amsterdam.

Rick Conrad is an experienced and skilled mountaineer and an enthusiastic researcher and writer on the climbing scene. He is co-author of the book, *Climb to Glory: The Adventures of Bill Hackett*, the life story of a world-traveled Portland mountaineer and veteran of the 10th Mountain Division's Italian Campaign. Besides mountaineering, Ric Conrad is deeply committed to his duties in the Naval Reserve, in which he served as a junior officer aboard a ship in the Middle East conflict.

About the Author

 **Dee Molenaar** was born in Los Angeles in 1918 to Dutch immigrant parents, who enjoyed taking their two sons and daughter on hikes in the Hollywood Hills and exploring the local seashores, deserts, and mountains of Southern California. Almost inseparable in their childhood and youth, Dee and his younger brother Cornelius, whom they called K, later extended their climbing horizons to the glaciered volcanoes of the Pacific Northwest, where they began many years of close association with Mount Rainier as summit guides and park rangers.

In 1930, the Eastman Kodak Company celebrated its 50th anniversary in the film and camera business by giving the first 500,000 twelve-year-old kids in the United States (whose parents would take them to the corner drugstore to pick it up) the Golden Anniversary model of its Brownie box camera. This got Dee started in photography at an early age, and he has since seldom been without a camera during his many travels through the mountains and deserts. During World War II, Dee served as a photographer in the U.S. Coast Guard in the Aleutian Islands and Western Pacific, while his brother K served in the 87th Mountain Infantry Regiment on Kiska and in the Italian Campaign.

After the war, the Molenaar brothers took advantage of the GI Bill at the University of Washington, and both earned their bachelor's degrees with majors in geology. In 1954, after serving for a few years as a park ranger at Mount Rainier National Park and, briefly, as a civilian advisor in the Army's Mountain and Cold Weather Training Command at Camp Hale, Colorado, Dee began his career in geology. He worked for Phillips Petroleum Company in Alaska, Colorado, and Utah; the Washington Department of Conservation in Olympia; and the U.S. Geological Survey in Tacoma, from which he retired in 1983.

Back in the Pacific Northwest, Dee continued actively exploring, climbing, and guiding on nearby Mount Rainier and its surrounding foothills. After climbing the mountain some fifty times via fifteen different routes, including three first ascents, Dee authored the award-winning book *The Challenge of Rainier,* a definitive work published in 1971 by The Mountaineers Books that is now in its ninth updated printing.

Dee has climbed peaks throughout the western United States, Alaska, Canada, the Alps, and the Himalayas, and has hiked in the Andes, New Zealand, and Antarctica. He participated in major expeditions to Mount St. Elias in Alaska in 1946 and in the ill-fated 1953 American expedition to K2 in the Karakoram Range, adjacent to the Himalayas. These were followed by a couple of mini-expeditions to Mount McKinley in 1960 and Mount Kennedy in the Yukon in 1965. His field research in preparing and self-publishing several artistically rendered landform maps has taken him on geology- and map-oriented treks to Mount Everest, Machu Picchu in the Peruvian Andes, and the McMurdo Sound area of Antarctica, the latter travel supported by a grant from the National Science Foundation.

Besides his ever-present cameras, an important part of Dee's climbing pack has been a small box of watercolors, with which he has painted mountain landscapes from elevations ranging from below sea level in Death Valley, California to a breathtaking 25,000 feet on K2. His paintings are in private collections throughout the United States, Canada, Alaska, Europe, New Zealand, China, and the former Soviet Union. Molenaar's pencil and ink sketches and maps appear in numerous mountaineering journals and magazines, and in guidebooks and autobiographies written by fellow mountaineers. Dee is an honorary member of The Mountaineers and The American Alpine Club and a life member of the Appalachian Mountain Club. In 2006, he was inducted into the Tacoma-Pierce County Sports Hall of Fame.

Dee and his wife, Colleen, live in southern Kitsap County, Washington, and have a daughter, two sons, and four grandchildren. In his retirement, Dee continues to work on art and map projects, in addition to writing and lecturing about his mountaineering travels and geologic observations.

Index